SMART

MARKETING

---

52 Brilliant Tips & Techniques to Boost Your Profits and Expand Your Business

By
Jeff & Marc Slutsky

CAREER PRESS
3 Tice Road
P.O. Box 687
Franklin Lakes, NJ 07417
1-800-CAREER-1
201-848-0310 (NJ and outside U.S.)
Fax: 201-848-1727

Copyright © 1998 by Jeff & Marc Slutsky

SMART MARKETING
Cover design by Design Solutions
Printed in the U.S.A. by Book-mart Press

To order this title, please call toll-free 1-800-CAREER-1 (NJ and Canada: 201-848-0310) to order using VISA or MasterCard, or for further information on books from Career Press.

Library of Congress Cataloging-in-Publication Data

Slutsky, Jeff, 1956-
      Smart marketing : 52 brilliant tips & techniques to boost your profits and expand your business / by Jeff & Marc Slutsky.
          p.   cm.
      Includes index.
      ISBN 1-56414-361-9 (hc.). -- ISBN 1-56414-362-7 (pbk.)
      1. Marketing.   I. Slutsky, Marc.   II. Title.
HF5415.S573   1998   98-20877
658.8--dc21

Dedication

To our children, Amanda, Mitchell, Austin, and Justin.

Contents

Introduction

Smart Marketing is a series of clever, shrewd, and smart tips, hints, and anecdotes that allow you to get more out of your business with less money. You'll discover the inside tricks and techniques from some of the most successful and creative people from around the world. It's presented in a vignette-like format that is sure to keep you interested, motivated, and mesmerized.

Smart Marketing provides you with 52 short chapters, one for each week of the year. The topics are in all areas of marketing, advertising, promotion, customer service, and sales and are applicable to many types of businesses. The goal of the book is to provide an understanding of how to run a more profitable business. We suggest that each week you read one chapter. Then spend a little time applying the information from that chapter to your specific business. Your success will come from the adaptation of these ideas to your needs and unique opportunities.

A "Smart Marketing action plan" is provided at the end of each chapter to help you convert the ideas into action. Some of the ideas will be more readily adaptable to your business than others, yet you'll find that most of these ideas, if given the proper development, will help you become more successful in your business. Use these 52 chapters as "thought starters." We want to get you thinking more creatively about your business. But it is your job to take the ideas to the next level. Modify. Adapt. Improve. Make them work for you.

We have conducted many consulting and training programs throughout the country for a variety of businesses, large and small, including McDonald's, Goodyear, Marriott, Minit Lube, Exxon, Molson, and many others. We start with the basics of Smart Marketing, and in every situation, we develop the ideas further so that they work for their individual dealers, franchisees, managers, or stores. You can use this book to help you do the same thing.

—Jeff and Marc Slutsky

Chapter 1

In Selling, All the World's a Stage

You can dramatically increase your communications effectiveness by applying some techniques commonly used by professional actors, according to Ellen Kaye, a New York-trained professional actress. Her Scottsdale, Arizona-based company, Perfect Presentations, is a presentation, communication, and image consulting organization that transforms many Fortune 500 executives into more effective presenters and leaders.

Drawing upon her experiences as one of the top actors in New York, Ellen explains that actors are trained to convince *you* of *their* "reality." She learned certain mental and emotional exercises that helped her to convince millions that she had a pounding headache, when she really didn't; or that she was having the "time of her life" with Kathie Lee and Frank Gifford on a Carnival Cruise®, when she really had a pounding headache. Likewise, you can use those same brain drills just prior to visiting a customer, colleague, or boss to help you get past those emotional blocks that zap your effectiveness. When you walk through the door for an important meeting, it is as if the camera is rolling during a major shoot.

Emotional memory

When you're selling, you have to be at your best whether you feel like it or not. Just before a scene, actors often briefly visualize a pleasant experience from their past. Ellen suggests that just before an important meeting, close your eyes and recall how good you felt during a special experience. Then open your eyes and charge forward with the same feeling fresh in your mind.

Substitution

This acting technique is used in many different ways, including when actors have a challenge working with another actor. For example, it's very difficult to show the proper emotion during a love scene when the person with whom you're pretending to be head over heels makes you feel just the opposite. To get into character, the actor might mentally substitute the undesirable partner with one he or she does like. In selling or managing, you may have to have a good working relationship with people who are difficult. So next time you find yourself in this situation, mentally substitute a person you like for the one you dislike.

Immediate previous circumstance

Actors know that their entire outlook and emotional state leading up to the next scene is determined by events that just happened. If you're heading into an important meeting or making a critical sales presentation, and you just found out your company announced a major restructuring, you may have difficulty being persuasive. Ellen suggests that you recall a positive previous circumstance immediately before your presentation or meeting. For example, most salespeople like to celebrate after a big sale.

That's a waste of a powerful immediate previous circumstance. The time to go after a big sale is right after you've made one. Your immediate previous circumstance is so positive that you stand a much better chance of getting another sale.

Smart Marketing action plan

1. Write down three very positive experiences you've had this past year.

2. Practice "emotional memory" with each one to see which memory works best for you.

3. Write down two of your favorite clients or colleagues.

4. Practice "substitution" with two difficult clients or colleagues.

5. To create a positive "immediate previous circumstance" before an important meeting, recall a specific event in which you had the feeling you need now.

6. Contact Perfect Presentations for a free copy of Ellen Kaye's *10 Acting Tips for Executives* at 602-314-0888.

Chapter 2

Turning Complaints Into Compliments

"Seven out of 10 complaining customers will do business with you again if you resolve the problem in their favor," according to Dr. Michael LeBoeuf, author of *How to Win Customers and Keep Them for Life*. "If you resolve that complaint on the spot, 95 percent will do business with you again. On average, a satisfied complainer will tell five people about the problem and how it was satisfactorily resolved."

However, if you don't handle the complaint appropriately, then not only do you lose that customer's business, but the dissatisfied customer will tell eight to 10 people about the problem. So, it is very important that you not only treat your customers right, but when they complain, it's imperative that you handle it promptly and politely.

Wilting customer service

LeBoeuf told us of a florist named Bob who received an angry phone call from one of his customers. Apparently Bob mixed up a couple of orders. He accidentally sent an arrangement to celebrate the grand opening of a new branch office that read, "Rest in Peace." When the customer angrily complained to the florist about receiving the wrong floral arrangement, Bob replied, "You think you're upset; on the other side of town some dearly departed just received a wreath that says, "Good Luck in your new location."

From gripe to gratification

When you treat your customers like Bob did, you're losing out on earning that customer's business back. Not only that, if you resolve your customer's complaint promptly and to the customer's satisfaction, your customer will feel better about your business than if there were no problems to begin with. Remember, when a customer complains, it means that you are not living up to your customer's expectations. And if you don't, some other business will probably get the opportunity to prove that they can. It is important to listen to those complaints, because you will discover possible areas where you need improvement. It gives you another chance at correcting the problem, plus when the problem is corrected, you will earn that customer's loyalty and keep that customer from shopping the competition.

Each time you come in contact with a customer, it is a *moment of truth,* according to Dr. LeBoeuf. When that moment of truth is a customer's complaint, he suggests you follow these simple rules:

- Listen carefully to the customer's complaint. It helps to defuse anger and to demonstrate your concern.

- Paraphrase and record what he or she tells you. Say something like, "Let me make sure I have this straight..."

- Find out what the customer wants (for example, a refund, a credit, or a discount).

- Propose a fair solution and get his or her support. "If I take it back and give you full credit, would that be okay with you?"

- If he or she doesn't like your solution, ask him or her to propose one.

- Resolve the problem on the spot, if possible.

- Where appropriate, make a follow-up call to the customer.

- Never let the customer lose face.

Of course, some customers will take advantage of you. However, that is a small price to pay, because the majority of your customers will appreciate your efforts to serve their needs. As a result, you will be rewarded with their purchases and referrals for years to come.

Smart Marketing action plan

1. Create a policy to resolve customer complaints on the spot whenever possible.

2. Empower your employees with the authority to resolve complaints when they occur (that is, accept exchanges, offer refunds, give freebies, etc.).

3. Make sure your resolutions are always in the favor of the customer.

4. If your solution is not acceptable to the customer, ask the customer to propose one, then work from there.

5. Most importantly, remember that while the customer may not always be right, "The customer is always the customer."

Chapter 3

Barter Club Benefits

Bartering your goods and services can be a smart way to pick up new customers and added sales, while getting some needed products or services for your business or personal use. But there are several challenges when you barter one-on-one:

- Finding a business that offers something you want, and that simultaneously wants what you have.

- Making an exchange of equal and fair value.

These problems are solved by joining a barter exchange club. Instead of the inconvenience of direct one-on-one barter deals, you buy with barter credits that you earn by selling your goods to other barter club members. But to maximize the increased profitability to your business with a barter club, you need to be smart in two areas:

1. Generating barter credits.

2. Spending barter credits.

In this chapter, you'll discover tips on *generating* barter credits. In the next chapter, you'll learn some inside tips for getting the most out of the credits when spending them.

"For every dollar of product or service one of our members sells to another barter club member, they get a dollar of credit in their barter account. They then use those earned barter credits to buy items from other members, which, in turn, allows them to cut overhead or enhance their life style," according to Mark Faber of Business Exchange International of Columbus, Ohio. He added, "With more than 500 members locally and more than 28,000 members nationally through 140 affiliated BXI offices, our members have used their barter credits to buy and sell just about everything from printing, painting, plumbing, and programming, to piñatas, puppies, pools, and pizzas." (We then pondered if perhaps one of their participants was Peter Piper.)

Provide good service

Unfortunately, a small number of businesses treat barter customers with less enthusiasm than cash customers. They forget that a club member purchase is an opportunity to build a loyal customer. For example, we were very pleased with our barter club florist. Now, in addition to all of our local barter business, that florist picked up our out-of-town cash business, as well.

Member marketing

Take the marketing initiative by using inexpensive or free barter club group mailings, inserts, networking lunches, broadcast fax promotions, newsletters, etc. Once members learn about you, they often will go out of their way to buy from you, rather than a nonbarter competitor.

Make it easy to buy

It's generally understood that direct costs, such as sales tax, tips, and shipping charges, are paid in cash. However, to attract more barter sales, especially with bigger-ticket items, consider allowing members to pay for the entire purchase with barter. Of course, you owe the sales tax in cash to the state, but if your profit margin is high enough, the small increase in your cost of taking 100-percent barter for the entire purchase should be more than covered by increased sales.

Smart Marketing action plan

1. List your high-profit products and services.

2. Contact a barter exchange club, such as BXI, to determine their members' level of demand for your high-profit items.

3. Ask to see a list of members and call several for their feedback on the effectiveness of their barter program.

4. Have the barter club sales representative clearly explain the costs and fees involved for membership and transactions.

5. Once you join, become proactive in promoting your company to the membership.

Chapter 4

Getting the Most from Your Barter Credits

Joining a barter club can be a good way to pick up new customers and added sales, while getting needed products or services in return. With your barter credits, which you learned how to accumulate in the last chapter, you'll want to be very smart about how you spend them, so that you realize the maximum benefits for your business.

Half and half

It's generally accepted then when you use barter credits, you charge "full retail to full retail." However, because most businesses often offer deals, discounts, and coupons, you may find that you're paying a premium when buying with barter credits. However, we have found that some will match our regular vendor's price when we offer to pay with half cash and half barter.

Clearing house

Another way to use a barter club is as an incentive to increase the size of your customer's purchase. For example, several years ago, we did a big training project for a major tire manufacturer. They then wanted to add an extra day to the program but didn't have any more money in the budget. So we took the extra fee in tires. Soon our office was filled with tires, and because we didn't need all of them, we turned them over to Mark Faber at BXI, a local barter exchange club. He, in turn, sold them to his members for barter credits, which we then used to buy office supplies, as well as Marc's new patio, Jeff's apartment rent, a sushi dinner for eight, bikes for the kids, and neutering for two cats.

Be a hero

If you have a bunch of barter bucks accumulated and don't really want to spend them for your business, you might donate them to a nonprofit group, such as the American Cancer Society (ACS). ACS and other worthy causes can use your credits to help offset the costs of running their organizations. And because the IRS doesn't distinguish between barter dollars and regular dollars, our brother Howard Slutsky, CPA (who got his carpet cleaned and his new pickup rustproofed on barter), says that you would be able to write that off as a cash donation.

Employee benefit program

The barter club can open up "sub accounts" for your employees. You can then transfer barter credits to their personal accounts when they win sales or productivity contests. Or if your sales force generates barter sales for you, you can pay their commission in barter credits. The employees can then spend the credits any way they want to. You can also use your barter credits to give your employees gift certificates to area restaurants, gift baskets, massage/manicure packages, trips, or even a catered employee party.

Smart Marketing action plan

1. Review the previous chapter on accumulating barter credits.

2. Identify those expenses in your business that could be offset using barter credits.

3. Before switching to barter vendors, first compare price, quality, and service with that of your regular vendors.

4. Test the new barter vendor with a small percentage of your business. If it does a good job, you can begin to increase its share of your business.

5. If there is a vendor from whom you want to buy using barter, contact your barter club and suggest that it invite that business to join.

Chapter 5

Biz Blunders

Successful businesspeople learn from their mistakes. Making mistakes from taking risks is part of the educational process for any successful businessperson.

Ovary oops!

When a client returned to the vet to pick up his AKC-registered champion show dog, he noticed that his bill seemed awfully high for a bath and spray. So he mentioned that $100 seemed pretty pricey just to get his dog clean and flea-free. That's when he discovered that he was being billed for a bath and *spaying*. The lawsuit that followed basically rendered the vet financially neutered. We don't know if the client ever got rid of the fleas. *Lesson:* Give your customers what they want.

Sweet surprise

We were recently told of a new kosher-style deli that was having problems with their young servers because they just weren't familiar with the product line. One customer ordered a Reuben sandwich on *challah*. Challah (pronounced hǎʹlǎ) is traditional Jewish, braided bread. When his ordered arrived, his sandwich was on *halavah* (pronounced hǎʹlǎ vǎʹ), which is a very sweet, candy-like dessert. *Lesson:* Before you let your employees serve your customers or clients, make sure they understand the products and services you offer.

Chicken feed

Making mistakes is part of doing business. The key is to learn from those experiences. We've had our share of biz blunders over the years. Marc was the volunteer chairperson for an ad hoc committee of a nonprofit organization. The problem was that he couldn't get his committee members to attend the meetings, and this was taking up more of his time than he anticipated. He had only one scheduled meeting left. He wanted to insure that a quorum would be present so that they could vote on their final recommendation, and then he'd be free of this task once and for all.

To motivate his committee members to attend, he mailed out a flier that promised them a *free chicken dinner* at the end of the meeting. Everyone showed up. After the vote, he treated them to their free chicken dinner—little packets of dried corn! *Lesson:* Don't do this.

Insensitive situation

Then there was the fast food franchise owner who was so proud of his new Braille menu, that he had it laminated. *Lesson:* Use a little common sense.

Smart Marketing action plan

1. Make a list of between five and 10 of the biggest mistakes you've made in your business or career.

2. For each one, write down the most important lesson you learned as a result of this mistake.

3. Write out what changes you've made (or will make) as a result of that experience.

4. If you have less than three mistakes, consider taking a little more risk.

Chapter 6

Marketing With Business Cards

You can easily turn an inexpensive business card into a powerful marketing tool. All you have to do is, two to three times a day, hand it out to someone who is not your customer or client. Start with those people with whom you already come in contact. When you're doing errands, for example, you may encounter the waiter at the local restaurant, the grocery store clerk, your hair stylist, mail person, dry cleaner, or even the police officer giving you a warning to slow down. The list is endless. Simply hand out your card, introduce yourself, and invite the person to become your customer or client.

Free cup of coffee creates new customers

Barbara is the manager of a convenience store in Parkersburg, West Virginia. During an 11-week period, she passed out 200 business cards to people she did not recognize as being her customers. On the back of her cards she wrote, "Free regular soft drink or coffee," and then she signed them. She told her potential customers that when they came into her convenience store, the soft drink was on her. Of the 200 she passed out, 51 came back—more than a 25-percent return rate. Obviously, most of those who came in and redeemed the card bought other things. Plus, many of those customers came back for more visits.

Hindsight promotion

A very successful stockbroker on the East Coast used a different version of business card distribution, according to Murray Raphael, author of *The Great Brain Robbery*. While commuting to work, this stockbroker had to pay several tolls. Before he paid a toll, he first looked in his rearview mirror. If he saw an upscale car, he not only paid his toll but also the toll of the person in the luxury car behind him. He then asked the toll booth attendant to hand his business card to the person in the car behind him, after writing a brief note on the back of the card. The note read, "If you think this is an interesting way of getting your attention, think of all the things I could do for your financial portfolio." He got many new clients off of a simple 90-cent toll and a clever use of his business card.

Smart Marketing action plan

1. Get 1,000 business cards printed.

2. Pass out at least 20 business cards each week to potential new customers or clients.

3. As you pass out your business card, introduce yourself and ask the person to become your customer.

4. If appropriate, provide an incentive. Handwrite an offer (a discount, value added, or small free offer) on the back of the card that encourages prospects to try you for the first time.

5. Track your results to see how many customers come back for another visit.

6. When your 1,000 business cards are gone, print another 1,000 and repeat steps 1 through 5.

Chapter 7

Creative Sales Calls Help Clients Remember

When your prospective buyers are tough to find, you might consider using some creativity in your sales approach to gain their attention. Consider the challenge of a pharmaceutical representative. She's in a very competitive sales job, where success depends on a combination of persuasive communication skills and tremendous technical knowledge. In her territory, there are dozens of representatives selling many different competitive products. The rep strives to build a long-term relationship with doctors, and it's a big advantage to get the doctors to associate the rep's name with the drugs.

Birth of an idea

This talented rep had a unique opportunity to set herself apart from the competition when her first child was born. She created a special birth announcement, just for the doctors in her territory. The rep represented three different drugs—a blood pressure drug, a cholesterol-lowering drug, and an antibiotic drug. To get the doctors' attention, the birth announcement was printed on a single sheet of blue paper, and featured the brand names of the three drugs she represented.

We would like to announce
the birth of our son
AUSTIN RYAN
Born Friday, October 22, at 12:18 a.m.
Weight: 6 lbs. and 15 oz.
Length: 19½ inches

Blood pressure: 70/50
Does not need:
[name of blood pressure medicine]

Cholesterol: LDL 100/HDL 55
Does not need:
[name of cholesterol medicine]

No staph, no strep, no UTI
Does not need:
[name of antibiotic]

She sent out 200 of these birth announcements, along with a photo of herself and the baby. She was surprised at the high number of physicians who displayed the birth announcement and pictures on their bulletin boards. Many of the competitors' reps made comments to her about seeing the announcement around the doctors' offices. In fact, several years later, a number of doctors still had it up in their offices.

Obviously, using a birth announcement has very limited application. But the idea behind the announcement offers you some real benefits if you adapt this idea to your needs. Your challenge is to come up with your own unique ideas that are specific to your business and your customers and that could provide a similar impact.

X-ray vision

Another sharp drug rep had difficulty getting one of his doctors to review the literature on one of his new products. So, he had the flier transferred to an x-ray and delivered to the doctor's office in the standard oversized envelopes used for transporting x-rays. It was read.

Smart Marketing action plan

1. Create a list of 25 prospective clients with which you wish to build a long-term relationship.

2. Identify something about your prospects and your product or service that you can use to get the prospect to notice you and what you sell. Keep it very simple.

3. Combine that idea with your product or service into a creative sales or marketing approach. You can mail it or deliver it in person.

4. Follow up with the prospects to get an indication of the impact that idea made.

5. Do a promotional "post mortem." Try to figure out ways to improve on the idea even more.

6. Modify and test those creative ideas to work with other prospects.

7. Temper your creativity with common sense. Be careful not to try something so "creative" that it might backfire by offending or upsetting your prospect.

Chapter 8

Challenge Employees to Bring You Business

A surefire way to keep your employees enthused, motivated, and hustling to bring you business is to have an employee contest. This is how it works:

Design your own "special value" card. This card entitles the bearer to a special savings or value added at your business. Be sure to include an expiration date. On a voluntary basis, your employees, both full- and part-time, receive 50 cards each.

**Now You Have a Friend at
[Insert Your Business Name]!**

This card entitles the bearer to receive:

[Insert Value or Savings]

**Cannot be combined with any other offer or savings.
Only one card per person. Offer expires 00/00/98**

Authorized by_____
Valued employee

The card has a place for the employee's signature to authorize the offer. By using his or her signature, your employee feels special, knowing that he or she is a valued part of the success of your business.

Once the value cards have been printed and handed out to all participating employees, then the contest begins. Their goal is to distribute these cards to family, friends, and acquaintances in their neighborhoods. If any of the participants need more than 50 cards each, give them more.

The rules

1. The cards are to be handed out to *new* customers only.
2. Distribution of the cards must be done on the employees' own time.
3. Distribution takes place beyond the perimeter of your parking lot.

Occasionally, you will find an employee who might take advantage and break one of the rules. That is a no-no. You can deal with each situation in your own special way.

Tracking results

Count the total number of cards redeemed. Whichever employee has the most cards redeemed is the winner, the person with the second most takes second place, and so on.

Prizes

The prizes are essential to making this contest fun and to motivating your employees to participate. Many of the prizes can be bartered with other area businesses, including car washes, CDs, movie passes, movie rentals, dinners, etc.

It is very important that every active participant win something, even if only one card is redeemed. You could also have weekly winners, and then at the end of the contest, a grand prize winner. The grand prize should be something a little more valuable, such as a small color TV, boom box, or gift certificate in the $50 to $100 range. However, the most popular grand prize we've discovered is generally the least costly: a day off with pay.

The contest should last one month. Also, the cards should be passed out in the first week of the contest.

Smart Marketing action plan

1. Design a special value card that offers a savings or value added at your business. This should be more of a value than a typical sale offer or coupon.

2. Give each employee 50 special value cards that he or she can pass out to family and friends. (If some employees want more, give them more.)

3. On a voluntary basis, employees pass out these cards on their own time, away from your business.

4. Keep track of the value cards. Show only the rankings, not the actual numbers, on a poster board, so employees can see where they stand in the contest.

5. Have weekly prizes and a grand prize at the end of the month. Anyone who participates wins something.

6. Repeat the contest six months later.

Chapter 9

Ethics Gap Creates a Big Dilemma

"Good ethics is good for business," according to Frank Bucaro, an Elgin, Illinois-based speaker and trainer on business ethics and values. The big problem is what Frank calls an *ethics gap,* which is the difference between what is moral and what is good for business. If you strive to be ethical in business, it will pay you back in the long term. Frank further added, "And just because it's legal doesn't mean it's ethical." For long-term success, positive word-of-mouth is often the best form of marketing. Your reputation determines whether customers will continue doing business with you and will refer others.

Ethical or pathetic?

Frank gave his ethical opinion on several examples.

- **Opening volley.** An appliance store owner was faced with a major competitor opening a new location just down the street. The competitor spent a lot of money advertising its big grand opening. Knowing that many people would be driving past his store on the way to the grand opening, the store owner decorated his parking lot with balloons, pennants, a clown by the street waving people in, and a big sign that read, "Now Open."

Many of the people ended up in his store instead of the new competitor's.

Ethics by Frank: Okay by me. No one was forced to visit the store.

- **Competitor's customer list.** There were two competing night clubs. One owner wanted a list of his competitor's customers for targeted mailing. He knew that there was a health club that set out free drawings at different businesses. He offered a special incentive to put one in the competitor's night club. The health club manager then gave him the box after the contest was over. All the forms that were left contained the names, addresses, and phone numbers of the competitor's customers.

Ethics by Frank: No way. The list was generated using false information and deception.

- **More competition.** A fast food restaurant, part of a major chain, was the only player in a small community on the East Coast. Without competition, this unit was doing a sales volume of almost twice the national average for that chain. Another fast food chain decided that it would be a perfect market to open up one of its units. It built the unit right next door to the first restaurant. It spent a lot of money on the grand opening, figuring that it could shave off 30 to 40 percent of the market. That would be a very successful unit. On the day of the grand opening, the first restaurant put up a sign that said, "In honor of our new neighbors, we will be closed. Go visit them."

The new competitor was not expecting a 100-percent market share that day. Because one of the main reasons to go to a fast food restaurant is speed, many customers were upset. People were waiting in line for hours. Food was prepared poorly and certain items were not even available. That new competitor lasted only several months because of the bad reputation acquired at its grand opening.

Ethics by Frank: No problem. No one was forced or coerced into visiting the new competitor. Unlike the previous example, there was no deception.

Smart Marketing action plan

To help insure that you're making an ethical decision, follow Frank Bucaro's four steps:

1. Understand the specific action you're planning to take.

2. Identify the circumstances leading up to this action.

3. List the criteria you're using for making this judgment.

4. Communicate your intent with several people you trust, and get their feedback.

Chapter 10

Competitive
Exit Strategies

When a competitor decides to shut its doors, there may be an opportunity knocking at yours. Consider the private investigator in Akron, who was able to take advantage when one of his major competitors went out of business. The competitor had a half-page yellow page ad. The private investigator found out that the competitor used an answering service and that the service owned the phone number listed in the ad. So, he took over the competitor's nominal monthly answering service fee. As a result, he doubled his sales for less than $50 a month.

A major pizza franchise had a competitor literally right next door that went out of business. The franchise owner was able to buy the competitor's unused number from the local phone company by simply adding an additional line to his phone system.

Sewing up his competition

Bob Kramer of Kramer's Sew & Vac in Cincinnati achieved a similar goal, but with a different approach. When one of Bob's competitors went out of business, its phone service was terminated. Calling that number, potential customers were informed that the number was no longer in service. Bob paid the competitor $100 to contact the phone company and tell them to have their computer announce a number change instead of a disconnect. The new number that was given out was Bob's!

This is one of those ideas that may not work every time, but it's certainly worth a shot. The worst that can happen is that the competitor won't let you do it. But if it works, it can be a nice jump in your inbound calls.

A super idea

Some Super 8 Motel franchisees had an interesting problem that was brought to our attention when we did a workshop at their annual convention. Apparently, customers would confuse them with Motel 6 and often would call directory assistance asking for "Motel 8." After about 10 minutes of brainstorming with the group, we decided that the solution was to place an additional listing in the phone book under "Motel 8" at a minimal monthly charge. If your customers are going to ask for you by a certain name, you should make it easy for them to find you.

Let your fingers walk the talk

No matter how proud you are of your yellow page ad, it's not a good idea to advertise, "Look for our ad in the yellow pages" in your other advertising. It's the only advertising medium that puts your ad next to all of your competition. That makes it too easy for your customers to use the phone and price shop you to death. Make your yellow page advertising work on its own.

Smart Marketing action plan

1. Keep your eyes open for competitors that are announcing that they're going out of business.

2. Approach the competitor if it's a local independent business, and see if it will ask the phone company to announce a number change (to your number).

3. If the competitor agrees, you might also try to buy its customer database.

4. Offer to buy your competitor's "out of business" banner if you can also put "go to (your business)" on the banner.

5. If your competitor doesn't cooperate, contact the phone company yourself and try to buy the competitor's number and add a new line to your phone system.

6. Look for other variations of your company name to create additional listings that would position you near your competition in the white pages and in directory assistance.

Chapter 11

Just the Fax

There are several interesting ways you can turn your fax machine into a powerful sales and marketing tool.

Broadcast fax

Most fax machines have the ability to *broadcast* the same message to many different locations once the fax numbers have been programmed into the machine. Stand-up comic and professional speaker, Dale Irvin, from Downers Grove, Illinois, faxes his *Friday Funnies* to more than 200 meeting planners, clients, and colleagues. Every Friday, people who could hire or refer him receive his single-page mini-newsletter of quips, wit, and humor, showcasing Dale's talents.

When Dale is talking to a prospective client, he asks if they want to receive his *Friday Funnies*. He recommends that you get permission to put someone on a broadcast fax list. He also gets more mileage from the same fax by providing it free, as an added value, for those people who buy a subscription to his monthly newsletter, *Funny Business*.

Why did Dale choose Fridays? Because his long distance service offers Fridays free! If you would like a free sample of *Friday Funnies*, call Dale at 630-852-7695 and tell him that the Slutskys sent you.

Delayed transmission

We followed Dale's lead by faxing our weekly business column *BizSmart* to key prospects, clients, and colleagues in those markets that don't get our column. Unfortunately, we don't get Fridays free, like Dale. So we program our fax machine to transmit the single-page article at midnight on Mondays (the day it comes out in Columbus), which is when we get the lowest rate. We have nearly 70 locations on our list, and it takes just under two hours to complete.

The urgent fax

Hal Becker, a Cleveland-based sales trainer and author of *Can I Have Five Minutes of Your Time?*, suggests that you use your fax machine to get decisions from prospects who stop returning phone calls, despite repeated attempts. We affectionately refer to this fax as our "poop-or-get-off-the-pot fax." On a fax cover sheet we put:

> I'm in a bind and I need your help! Please check one of the following, and fax it back to me as soon as it is completed. Your prompt response is truly appreciated.
>
> _____ **Yes,** I want the Street Fighter program. Please send me the speaking agreement.
>
> _____ **Not quite sure.** Street Fighter is still under consideration. I have some questions. Call me back on _____ at _____.
>
> _____ **No,** I don't want the Street Fighter program at this time. Please call back on _____ at _____ to stay in touch.

We've found that Hal's fax technique gets us about a 90-percent response rate, which divides almost equally among the three choices. It's an effective way to find out exactly where you stand with that potential sale.

Smart Marketing action plan

1. List the fax numbers of clients with whom you want to stay in contact regularly.

2. Create the format for a single- (or double-) sheet, content-rich, faxable mini-newsletter.

3. Ask your clients and colleagues if they would like to be on your fax list to receive this information.

4. Program your fax machine, or your computer fax server, to broadcast fax your mini-newsletter.

5. If you are faxing long distance, use the delayed transmission function to fax at times when your rates are the cheapest.

Chapter 12

Getting Past the Gatekeeper

All your sales techniques are worthless unless you can talk with the decision-maker. However, in many selling situations, there is a buffer or filter that keeps you from talking with the person who has the authority to make a buying decision. That obstacle could be a secretary, an assistant, or some other "gatekeeper." Gatekeepers are very dangerous, because they have the ability to say no but not the ability to say yes. When talking with gatekeepers, it is important to give them as little information as you can. The less they know, the better off you are.

Several tactics that allow you to sneak by the gatekeeper to the decision-maker are best explained using football as an analogy. You, the salesperson, are the high-powered offense, the decision-maker is the goal line, and the pesky gatekeeper is the defense. Here's one "play" to help you bypass the gatekeeper.

The run up the middle

This is your most direct approach, as you use your "verbal offensive line" to help you break through. A good gatekeeper asks you many questions before you're allowed to talk to the boss. The more questions you answer without getting "sacked," the closer you are to the goal. Respond to the question with a minimal amount of information, then follow up with *a call to action*. That call to action is a request to be connected to the person you're calling. Secretaries know that part of their job is to screen calls. Often, they do not feel they have done their job suitably unless they ask some questions. They may feel that the more questions they ask you, the better they are doing their job, despite how trivial some of those questions may be. Only after these secretaries are satified that they have done their job, do you stand a chance of getting through, assuming you gave no information that convinces them not to put you through to the decision-maker.

For example you might say, "This is Mitchell Nathan calling for Austin Ryan. Please put him on." Notice that it ends with a call to action.

"And who are you with?"

"I'm with Street Fighter Inc. Please tell Mr. Ryan I'm holding for him."

"Is he expecting your call?"

"I don't believe we have set up a specific time, but please let him know I am on the line."

"And what is it regarding?"

"Let Mr. Ryan know that I have the answers to the marketing questions."

"Does he know you?"

"You know, I don't think we have met personally, but I do have that information for him, so please let him know I'm holding for him."

Notice that Mitchell gave the very minimum information in answering each of the questions. The gatekeeper asked a lot of questions, so the caller was properly "screened." At the same time, Mitchell did not put the call in jeopardy by giving enough information to get disqualified.

Even with this technique, you can still get sacked, so you'll need some other plays. In the next chapter, you'll learn about *the end run*, *the reverse*, *the quarterback sneak*, and *the punt*.

Smart Marketing action plan

1. Make a list of the five or six most common questions gatekeepers ask you during phone calls.

2. Create a brief response to each that will not get you disqualified.

3. Write out different "calls to action" to follow those responses.

4. If the name of your company has a tendency to disqualify you, use an abbreviated version of it (i.e., Slutsky, Inc., instead of Slutsky Mutual Life, Inc.).

5. Track your success rate of getting past gatekeepers using the "run-up-the-middle" approach.

6. Never sell your product or service to the gatekeeper. Sell him or her only on putting you through to the decision-maker.

7. Read the next chapter for more plays.

Chapter 13

More on Getting
Past the Gatekeeper

In the last chapter, you learned that all your sales techniques are worthless unless you can talk with the decision-maker. However, in many selling situations, there is a buffer or filter that keeps you from talking with the person who has the authority to make a buying decision. That obstacle could be a secretary, an assistant, or some other "gatekeeper."

As mentioned in the last chapter, getting around the gatekeeper can be compared to a football game. Here are more "offensive plays" to help you bypass the gatekeeper.

The end run

Try reaching your prospect by calling a different department. If, for example, you want Mr. Jones in accounts payable, try calling shipping and asking for Mr. Jones. The person who answers will tell you that you've reached the wrong department. Ask him or her to transfer you to Mr. Jones's office. You may get transferred directly into his office.

The reverse

One approach that is particularly effective at times is to call the office of someone higher up in the organization.

If you are trying to reach the executive vice president, for example, call the chief executive officer's office. The CEO's secretary will inform you that you have reached the wrong office and will usually offer to transfer you to the right party. A call transferred from the boss's office stands a little better chance of getting through.

The quarterback sneak

Try calling very early in the morning. Often, busy executives get to the office by six or seven in the morning, long before their secretaries show up, so there is a very good chance that they will answer the phone themselves. Also try after work or on weekends. This play might also be successful at lunchtime, when the gatekeeper is gone and is replaced by a "bench warmer."

The bomb

The "bomb" requires that you break an earlier rule. You have tried everything and the only way you are even going to get a shot at the decision-maker is to sell the gatekeeper on the product or service. Chances for success are small, but if it is the only move you have left, you have to give it your best shot and lob the ball in the air.

The punt

Sometimes you have to cut your losses. There are many more prospects out there and if you cannot get through to this one after you have given it a good ole college try, move on. You might want to throw that lead into your "tickler file" and call back in five or six months.

Smart Marketing action plan

1. This week, make a commitment to make at least 50 telephone calls to prospective clients.

2. Try the end run, reverse, and the quarter back sneak at least 10 times each when your run-up-the-middle play doesn't score you a contact with your prospect.

3. Save the bomb and the punt for last resorts.

4. Track your results to see which plays work the best for you.

5. Continue the game plan with 50 calls a week, at least until the end of the season.

Chapter 14

Greeting Cards Build Loyalty

There are many advantages of using greeting cards to capture the attention of your hot prospects and to build loyalty with your existing customers and clients:

- They're relatively cheap.
- They're readily available at any card shop and many other stores.
- They're high-quality printed pieces.
- They're available in great variety.
- They almost always get opened and read.

In order to make an impact, you should use these greeting cards in unusual ways.

Giving thanks for their business

Scott Friedman, a professional speaker based in Denver, Colorado, told us, "I send out Thanksgiving cards in November, instead of Christmas and Hanukkah cards in December. All of my clients get tons of cards in late December, but they usually get only one Thanksgiving card a month earlier. And they remember my card more than all of the others."

Hair today and tomorrow

A hair stylist used greeting cards when he switched salons. Changing from the northern part of the city to a new salon just south of downtown, he was disappointed that 18 special customers didn't make the switch. Each month, he sent a different greeting card with the message, "I miss you." One month, he mailed only his business card with that same message on the back. Over the following 12 months, all 18 customers returned to his styling chair.

Let them know you love their business

Valentine's Day and, to a lesser degree, Sweetest Day are two opportunities to share your feelings with your customers and clients. The card should be on the light side. Be sure to write a note on the inside of the card, such as, "We love doing business with you," or "For a sweetheart of a deal, give us a call...." It's best to have the card signed by several key people in your organization or sign it from your business. (You don't want to give the wrong impression!)

Greetings for all occasions

Another idea is to have a small inventory of special greeting cards that you can use as the need arises. This would include "Condolences," "Get Well Soon," "Congratulations," "Happy Birthday," and "Happy Anniversary" (which can be used for wedding anniversaries or the anniversary of employment). A word of warning: If you're planning to use a wedding anniversary card for a client you haven't been in touch with for a while, it's a good idea to make sure that person is still married. It could be really embarrassing if you sent an anniversary card when you should have sent a condolence card or one of new congratulations.

When our first column of *BizSmart* came out, several of our key vendors had clipped it, put it in a "Congratulations" card and mailed it to us. It certainly was noticed! (But please, no more! Our mother has started a collection.)

You're the boss

Just when we got used to Sweetest Day, they came out with Boss's Day. Fortunately, *we* don't have to worry about that one. But there is an opportunity here. Think of the impact you would make sending a Boss's Day card to key customers or clients with the message, "You're The Boss."

Smart Marketing action plan

1. Buy three to four special-event greeting cards for each of the following: "Condolences," "Get Well Soon," "Congratulations," "Happy Birthday," and "Happy Anniversary."

2. Pick several holidays for which your customers would traditionally *not* get cards from vendors (Valentine's Day, Halloween, Thanksgiving).

3. Buy cards in quantity and send them to clients or customers with handwritten messages. Sign them from key people at your organization.

4. Think ahead. Buy cards after holidays to get a good price. A great time to buy Thanksgiving cards would be early December.

5. Next time you're out shopping, visit some card shops. Look at the cards for the different special occasions and think of specific clients they might appeal to, based on content (for example, a cartoon of a golfer for someone who golfs). Do some brainstorming.

Chapter 15

Value of Service Overcomes the Price Issue

Price is an important issue in the buying decision, but it's not the only issue. There are several other key elements that the majority of customers and clients consider before they make a commitment to buy, including a higher level of personalized service, more convenience, better quality, and greater selection, just to name a few. The only time price becomes the key concern to the consumer is when that customer does not perceive any difference between what you have to offer relative to your competition.

Ask yourself the question, "Why should someone pay you, say, 10 percent more for providing the same product as another business down the street?" Keep in mind that you can be competitively priced without being the lowest price, and that little extra margin you can get makes a big difference to your bottom line.

Take for example a hair salon on the West Coast. The owner built up a nice business. He learned all the newest styles, provided great customer service. He charged about $15 for a haircut, which was midrange for this market-place. Then a new shopping center opened up directly across the street, with a discount haircut franchise. To advertise this new location, the franchisee placed a billboard right in front of the new shopping center. With nothing but a plain blue background and plain white letters, the sign simply read, "We Give $6 Haircuts," and had a big arrow pointing into the shopping center.

Now all of these people who were going to their $15 haircut appointments saw the big billboard on the other side of the street advertising $6 haircuts. Seeking a bargain, a bunch of them went across the street to try it out.

So the hair stylist was losing business across the street because of price. What was he going to do? He could have cut his price in half and still not been competitive, based on price. Instead, this guy thought like a Smart Marketer. He rented his own billboard in front of his own salon. He used the same blue background and the same plain white letters, and his sign read, "We *Fix* $6 Haircuts." That turned him around instantly. Price is an issue, but it's not the only issue. And if your customers forget that you have something special to offer, you might just have to remind them.

Smart Marketing action plan

1. Do some comparison shopping to learn your competition's prices.

2. Identify those items or services that are of lesser quality than your competition's.

3. List those areas of your products or services where you provide better quality.

4. Write out several buyer benefits for those higher qualities.

5. Incorporate that information into your sales and advertising.

Chapter 16

Savvy Business Shoots Hole in One

We had a client who was approached by the organizers of a pro-amateur celebrity golf tournament about becoming one of 18 corporate sponsors. This was a major media event each year and the money was shared by 20 different charities. The cost of sponsorship was $750, which got you a sign on one of the holes and your company name mentioned in the program. Not a lot of exposure for your $750. He told them that this was such a worthy event that he wanted to do something special. He would put up a $10,000 cash prize for the first person to get a hole in one on the ninth hole; $5,000 would go to the golfer and $5,000 would be donated to the charity.

The organizers were ecstatic. This added a whole new dimension to the tournament. Tickets sales shot up and my client was interviewed on every TV and radio station. He had a fake check enlarged, complete with his logo, and displayed it on an easel at the ninth hole. The local newspaper took a picture of him standing next to it and it ended up on the front page. You couldn't buy that kind of publicity. He easily got more than $40,000 worth of free exposure. But there was some risk. What if someone got a hole in one? To protect himself in case anyone scored the hole in one, my client took out an insurance policy. Here's the funny part: The cost of the policy was only $450—$300 less than the sponsorship—and he totally dominated the tournament. Now think about it. Here are 17 other supposedly bright business people, each putting up $750 and getting zilch. And this Street Fighter puts up less money and owns the event!

We had lunch with him the day they made the announcement about the contest. Three very prominent people came up to him at different times during lunch and thanked him for his contribution to the community. After the third guy did this, he looked over to me and said, "Jeff, all I was trying to do was save $300!" It was so successful, he's done it every year since, and guess what happened last summer. That's right. Someone got the hole in one. Now, his premium may go up a little bit next year, but he doesn't care.

Smart Marketing action plan

1. Contact the National Hole In One Association at 800-527-6944 and get their information. They also have a basketball toss package.

2. Keep your eyes open for a golfing event that is well-organized and that supports a good local, noncontroversial cause.

3. Approach the organizers of the event about sponsoring a hole-in-one contest.

4. Make sure they publicize your contribution to the event. You may have to suggest approaches.

5. Look for inexpensive ways to leverage your effort (fliers or coupons for each participant, special signage, extra tickets to give your customers, having your company mentioned predominately on the marketing pieces, etc.).

6. If you sell a high-ticket item (such as cars, boats, apartments, etc.), use your product as the prize instead of cash.

Chapter 17

Hollywood-inspired Negotiations

Movies provide some of the greatest examples of effective negotiation tactics, according to Larry Winget, a Tulsa, Oklahoma-based motivational speaker. For example, in *Glengarry Glen Ross*, there's a scene where Al Pacino loses a sale because Kevin Spacey volunteers information in front of Pacino's client without knowing the details of the negotiations. Pacino later tells Spacey, "You never open your mouth until you know what the shot is." Winget says that you never volunteer unsolicited information, because it's often used in objections later on.

In *The Godfather,* Al Pacino's brother, James Caan (Sonny), was censured by his father, Marlon Brando (Vito Corleone), after they finished their meeting with Al Lettieri (Sollozzo). He tells his son, "Don't ever let the other person know what you're thinking." During that meeting, Sonny voiced interest in Sollozzo's idea to invest in narcotics, even though Vito was against it. Sonny's obvious interest lead to the attempted assassination of his father. Hopefully, making such a negotiation faux pas won't lead to such drastic measures in your mediations, but it could mean the death of your deal. It's better that you just "make them an offer they can't refuse."

Volunteering unsolicited information also got Mary McDonnell into trouble in *Sneakers*. Mary goes undercover by dating an employee at the corporate headquarters that Robert Redford's team breaks into. She's caught by Ben Kingsley, the computer-genius bad guy and the boss of the geek she's "dating." Ben buys her story at first and she's let go. As she is leaving, she casually mentions that she'll never go out on another computer date. Kingsley immediately determines that no computer would have matched those two, and her cover is blown. She should have followed the advice Jack Nicholson gave Karen Black in *Five Easy Pieces* when he said, "If you wouldn't open your mouth, everything would be just fine."

John Patrick Dolan, author of *Negotiate Like The Pros*, references *Weekend at Bernie's* in his seminars. Although "Bernie" is dead, nobody seems to notice. While propped up on a sofa at a party, dead Bernie receives an offer to buy his Porsche for $35,000. Bernie's silent. Minutes later, he's offered $40,000. Bernie says nothing. Then he's offered $45,000. Silence. Even with the offer tops $55,000, Bernie still says nothing. According to John, if we all acted more like Bernie, we'd put a lot more life into our negotiations.

When you move toward the end of the negotiations or the "close," you might follow the tactics presented by Paul Newman in *The Verdict*. He says, "Never ask a question unless you have the answer to it." When you get to the "closing" phase of negotiations, you're trying to get agreement. The only difference is that in a negotiation, the client is the judge and jury. One way to work toward a final "yes" is by asking a series of questions that will always get you a "yes." This movie quote points out a very important underlying element in successful negotiations, which is to simply do your homework before talking.

Smart Marketing action plan

1. Rent a number of your favorite movies.

2. As you're watching, look for scenes with effective negotiation tactics.

3. Write your favorite quotes on individual index cards and review them next time you start a negotiation.

4. Also look for quotes in other areas, such as customer service, leadership, time management, teamwork, etc.

Chapter 18

Hollywood-inspired Goal-setting

In the last chapter, you learned that movies can provide some great examples of effective negotiation tactics. Motivational speaker Scott McKain, author of *All Business Is Show Business*, told us that movies also teach us much about goal-setting. Scott, who co-hosts his own movie review show on WISH-TV in Indianapolis, referred to the original *Rocky* movie. Sylvester Stallone (Rocky Balboa) sets a very specific goal for himself. The night before the big fight he says, "I just wanna go the distance." There are several goal-setting lessons you can learn from this quote. The first is that you sometimes have to redefine "success."

In this scene, Rocky convinces himself that he can't win the fight, so he sets a new goal. By "going the distance," he can feel that he was a success because he achieved his goal. But it's possible that he might have just sold himself short. At least that would probably be the view presented in *Thelma and Louise* when Susan Sarandon (Louise) says, "Well, you get what you settle for."

If Rocky's goal was to beat Apollo Creed, he might have done just that. However, he never even gave himself a chance. Conversely, Apollo Creed set his goal when he said, "I'll drop him in six." This was after ignoring concerns from his trainer, who noticed Rocky's unusual training method of punching raw sides of beef. It seems that the message is that if you set a goal, you should first gather all the pertinent information about the project. Apollo did not reach his goal, even though he won the fight. Rocky lost the fight, but made his goal.

Unfortunately many people set their goals based on the fear of unrealized expectations. If Rocky had set his goal to beat Apollo and only went the distance, he might have felt like a loser. But because he was unwilling to take that emotional risk of setting his sights higher, he had to wait until *Rocky II* to finally beat Apollo.

But possibly the most poignant movie quote about setting goals was, "The road to genius is paved with fumble-footing and bumbling. Anyone who falls flat on his face is at least moving in the right direction...forward. And the fellow who makes the most mistakes may be the one who will save the neck of the whole world someday." It just seems kind of strange that this gem was said by Fred MacMurray in *Son of Flubber.*

Smart Marketing action plan

1. When setting goals, first gather all the pertinent information related to that goal.

2. Look at your goal from three perspectives: pessimistic, realistic, and optimistic.

3. Make sure your goal is attainable, yet challenging.

4. Set a reasonable deadline to reach the goal.

5. Create a step-by-step plan that illustrates how you intend to reach the goal.

6. As you move toward that goal, be flexible. Adjust it up or down as needed to maximize your performance.

Chapter 19

Don't Settle for Less

Two sisters were in the kitchen. One grabbed an orange, the only one left. The second sister exclaimed that she wanted the orange. They argued about it for several minutes and then came up with a solution. They agreed to cut the orange in half. This way, each sister got at least half of what she wanted. That sounds like a fair solution to the problem, but there was one element missing from this process: information.

As it turned out, the first sister wanted the orange to make fresh-squeezed orange juice. The second sister was baking and needed the orange peel for the recipe. Had they uncovered these pieces of valuable information at the beginning of their negotiations, both sisters could have gotten 100 percent of what they wanted, instead of settling for half.

Settling for far less than you have to in a negotiation is one of the most common results, according to John Patrick Dolan, JD, author of *Negotiate Like the Pros*.

John suggests that before you ever get to the negotiation table, do your homework. Gather as much information as you can about the people with whom you'll be negotiating. Here are some of the places John suggests you look:

- **Online.** Look for articles about the company or people. You may also find information in electronic directories, such as *Hoovers Handbook of American Business*. Also, look up their Web site for some company information.

- **The library.** Find articles, as well as other info. Most public companies, for example, will have their annual report on file at the library. Also look for hardcopy directories, such as *Who's Who*. You might also search their industry trade journals.

- **Telephone.** Be a customer and ask that brochures and background information about the company be mailed to you. You can also do a little telephone interview.

- **Credit check.** Subscribe to a service, such as Dunn & Bradstreet, and get a background check on the company. Also call the Better Business Bureau.

- **Public records.** There's a great deal of information available for the asking, if you ask the right people. Sometimes you may want the help of a professional to you get that information.

Once you begin your face-to-face negotiations, John suggests that you do more listening than talking. Ask a lot of open-ended questions. Those are the kind that usually begin with *what, why, where, who, when*, and *how*. If you want more details about a specific topic, follow with, "That's interesting. Tell me more." The more you can uncover of the "hidden agenda," the easier it will be for you to create a "100-percent win-win" situation.

Smart Marketing action plan

Here are 13 fatal negotiation mistakes you don't want to make:

1. Wanting something too much.
2. Believing that the other side has all of the power.

3. Failing to recognize your own strengths.
4. Getting hung up on one issue.
5. Failing to see more than one option.
6. Approaching negotiations with a win-lose mentality.
7. Short-term thinking that ruins long-term relationships.
8. Trying to squeeze out too much.
9. Accepting opinions, statements, and feelings as facts.
10. Accepting positions as final.
11. Believing that having more authority gives you more power.
12. Talking too much and listening too little.
13. Negotiating in haste.

Source: *Negotiate Like the Pros*, by John Patrick Dolan, JD, CPAE.

Chapter 20

In Networking Clubs, It's Refer or Resign

One way to increase business with only a small investment is by becoming an active member of a referral network or tip club. Jeff was recently the guest of our brother Howard, a CPA and treasurer of his local chapter of Network Professionals, Inc. Frank Agin, the regional director, told us, "NPI's Pittsburgh-based Eastern Region, is one of three. Nationally, we have more than 100 chapters and 2,000-plus members throughout Ohio, California, Florida, Pennsylvania, and Minnesota."

There are several benefits from membership:

• A consistent stream of qualified referrals.

• A stable of businesses you feel comfortable referring to your clients.

• An opportunity to develop business relationships for getting and giving feedback, insights, and tips about business management.

As a member of your chapter, you get exclusivity in one of 144 different business categories. According to Eve Peterson, executive director and a cofounder of NPI, "The

Smart Marketing

ideal size of a chapter is between 25 and 40 members." In Howard's chapter, they have members in different areas, including personal services (accounting, law, financial planning, real estate), business services (telecommunications, office supplies, banking, computer repair, advertising, signs, printing), health care (chiropractic, massage therapy, dentistry), and so on. Each member gives at least two qualified referrals a month. If you fall behind in your referrals, you pay a fine. If the gap persists, you're asked to leave and they fill your position with someone who can better benefit the membership with referrals.

In the meeting Jeff attended, the members generated 30 different leads. Eric Whittenburg, a lawyer, ran a structured and productive meeting. Leads were referred by filling out a three-part, carbonless business referral form. In every meeting, there's a 20-minute presentation by one member about his or her business. This helps members better understand how to refer business to that member. Also at the meeting Jeff attended, each member gave a very brief "live commercial" of his or her ideal qualified referral. Because the referring leads are "qualified," Frank Agin claims a better than 75-percent close rate on those referrals.

Another benefit of membership is that you develop relationships with other businesspeople in your chapter. Once you develop trust with members, you have a stable of businesspeople you know will do a good job for your clients and customers. In this way, you become a valuable resource to your clients. Besides, when you make a referral, one member said that she feels uncommon obligation to do everything possible to make that new customer happy, because the referring member is someone she's going to see each week.

Several members told Jeff that the social element of the club was a big advantage. Because they run their own small businesses, they don't get much interaction with other people at their level. The chapter provides them with a sounding board for ideas and a camaraderie with several other businesspeople with whom they share the same pressures, passions, frustrations, and growing pains.

Smart Marketing action plan

1. Contact a networking organization and get its material. You can contact NPI at 800-929-LEAD or http://www.npinet.com.

2. Interview some members, preferably in a similar service, and see how they feel they've benefited.

3. Decide if you would benefit from joining a club that has an opening for your service.

4. If membership makes sense but your service is already taken, consider helping to create a new club in your community.

5. Once you join, make a commitment to become an active member. Plan on attending weekly meetings.

Chapter 21

Newsletters for New Customers

Newsletters provide several advantages as an effective form of communication between you and your customers:

- They position you as an expert in your industry or profession.
- They provide total flexibility in format and frequency of distribution.
- They're relatively inexpensive to produce.

The main downside of creating your newsletter is finding the time to write it. To deal with this problem, Linda Kunuth of Paragon Management Associates, a dentist's consulting firm, suggests that her clients form a cooperative newsletter venture with other, noncompetitive doctors and other health care providers in their area. According to Linda, "A dentist might approach a chiropractor, optometrist, psychologist, nutritionist, and podiatrist." Each doctor would provide an article for each of the newsletters, giving readers useful information about the doctor's area of expertise.

Having other experts contribute to your newsletter makes your publication more valuable to your customers. Plus, you control the cover page and dominate positions in the newsletter. You can also leave space for important advertising messages about your products and services.

When you select contributors, select those who will also create a newsletter for their customer base. The articles you write for your newsletter can then be published in theirs, as well. In the previous example, you could easily get six times the distribution of your information to potential new customers.

Some newsletter guidelines

- **Keep the information newsworthy.** If you want your customers to read your newsletter, give them information they can use. Your readers don't care about a staff person's birthday. Provide helpful tips, money-saving ideas, ways they can be smarter consumers, and info on your product or service. You can get ideas from your own trade journals, articles, and online searches. If you use someone else's information, be sure to get permission to use it and quote the source.

- **Keep your articles short.** With today's harried life styles, less is more. Make your points succinctly.

- **Use a professional design and format.** You might want to hire a professional graphic artist to design your cover page. This is a one-time cost. Once it's designed, you can easily use any desktop publisher or word processor to do the rest.

- **Print a two-color cover for almost the price of one.** You can inexpensively add a second color to your cover page by "gang printing" the extra color for four or six editions at once. This requires that elements in your cover design remain constant for each newsletter (the newsletter name, logos, borders, etc.). Simply print the body copy in black for each edition, as needed.

Smart Marketing action plan

1. Create a simple newsletter format, perhaps a two-sided, 11" x 17" self-mailer.

2. Write short, information-packed articles that you know your readers will find valuable.

3. Contact between three and six noncompetitive associates or businesses that are complementary to your business or practice. Ask them to be contributors to your newsletters. You'll provide an "editor's note" with their name and phone number. Also see if they would be interested in doing a newsletter for their customers, and offer to return the favor with your articles.

4. Start on a biyearly or quarterly basis. If you want to increase frequency, do so by using "special editions" before making the commitment to go bimonthly or monthly.

5. See if your counterparts in other parts of the country are printing newsletters, and offer to "exchange" articles.

Chapter 22

Important
Telephone Opener

When you're making a business-to-business sales call over the telephone, you only have about 20 to 30 seconds to pique your prospect's interest. After that, you're talking to dial tone. Here's a four-step opener you can use:

1. Intro.
2. Benefit statement.
3. New news.
4. Permission to pursue.

1. Intro

The first step is to introduce yourself and your company or organization. For example, "This is Justin Ross of Street Fighter Marketing. Have you heard of us?" The purpose of the question is to involve the prospect immediately in your conversation. Of course, if your company is very well-known, you may want to modify the question.

2. Benefit statement

The second step tells your prospect the end result of having used your products or services. For example, ours is, "We specialize in teaching businesses how to advertise, promote, and increase sales without spending a lot of money." The usual response is, "No kidding, how do you do that?" Notice that there is no mention of seminars, speeches, consulting, books, or tapes. Your clients are interested in the value they can receive. How you provide that value are details best addressed later. (For more on benefit statements, see Chapter 47.)

3. New news

The third step is the new news, which is some new development or information that is so exciting you just had to get on the phone and share it with this prospect. You don't want something too specific that might get you disqualified. Keep it somewhat ambiguous. The one we use is, "We just created some new programs that our clients tell us get them tremendous results." What has the client learned about our services? Nothing! That's what we want. It creates interest, while at the same time, it doesn't give the prospect a reason to say that he or she isn't interested.

4. Permission to pursue

The fourth step is to ask another question. The purpose of this question is get the prospect's permission to continue with your sales presentation. Because there are so many bad telemarketing calls, most people have a tendency to say no. Because they're predisposed to say no, we create a question that gets the word *no* for answer, but gives us what we want. We, therefore, ask a *negative question:* "Is there any reason why you wouldn't want to know more about it?" If they say no, we continue with our presentation. And it's such a confusing question, that they can answer yes, and still mean no, but for you it's a signal to go on. So, anything short of "get lost," you can get some time with your prospect.

Smart Marketing action plan

1. Track the number of telephone presentations you currently give versus the number of calls you make.

2. Create your own four-step opener. Give special attention to your benefit statement.

3. Practice until it sounds natural and relaxed.

4. Test it on 10 "kamikaze" clients (ones who probably won't buy).

5. Use it on 10 good potential clients this week.

6. Refine your approach, particularly your benefit statement, and try again.

7. Study your improvement in the number of presentations given versus calls made.

Chapter 23

The Four
Personality Types

Whether selling a product or service to a customer or an idea to a colleague or employee, your results may be improved by first identifying which of the four basic personality types best characterizes that person. According to Cindy Kubica, an interpersonal skills speaker and trainer in Nashville, "The four personality types have been around since Hippocrates. It's been used and overused by countless sales trainers and management consultants." However, Cindy feels that she has simplified this complicated sales tool by describing each of the four types in terms of a character from the TV sitcom *Seinfeld*.

- **The Kramer.** Kramers are optimists, extroverts, thinkers, dreamers, and doers. They influence people with their enthusiasm. They have a tendency to be "big picture"-oriented and are more likely to shoot from the hip. When working with Kramers, don't give too many details. Help them "feel" and "envision" the final result. Other Kramers include Ralph Kramden (*The Honeymooners*), Fred Sanford (*Sanford & Son*), and Wile E. Coyote (*The Road Runner*).

• **The Elaine.** Elaines are dominating and directing. Like Kramers, Elaines are also doers, extroverts, and optimists. But they're more self-oriented and want to know as much about the process as the end result. They ruminate over decisions and often second-guess themselves. When selling to Elaines, give lots of details on how they will achieve their end result, step-by-step. Other Elaines include Larry Tate (*Bewitched*), Mr. Drysdale (*The Beverly Hillbillies*), and Mr. Spacely (*The Jetsons*).

• **The Jerry.** Jerrys are generally introverted, low key, and supportive. They have a tendency to be cautious and they like consistency. Jerrys become more like Kramers when they're in a totally safe environment (such as Jerry doing stand up). When selling to Jerrys, stress low risk, avoid pressure tactics, listen a lot, yada, yada, yada. Other Jerrys include Drew Carey, Sheriff Andy Taylor, and Scooby Doo.

• **The Newman.** Newmans are analyzing, conscientious, pessimistic, introverted, and action-oriented. When selling to Newmans, give them all the data. Show them charts and graphs. Use logic and limit emotions. Other Newmans include Felix Unger (*The Odd Couple*), Spock or Data (*Star Trek*), and Mr. Peabody (*Bullwinkle*).

What about **The George**? Cindy said that some personalities cross over between the four types. You get a George by extracting the worst traits of the other four. When possible, avoid Georges, get everything in writing, and get paid up front. Other Georges include Frank Burns (*M*A*S*H*), Ted Baxter (*The Mary Tyler Moore Show*), and The Trix Rabbit.

....

Joe Malarkey, a Norman, Oklahoma-based keynoter who bills himself as the *worst* motivational speaker in the world, presents his own satirical version, which he calls "Personality Types: The Three Hour Tour." Joe's unique interpretation uses characters from *Gilligan's Island*. Joe told us, "If you think my idea is ridiculous, then you guys are probably 'Professors!' "

Smart Marketing action plan

1. Make a list of 10 clients (or employees) you work with on a regular basis.

2. Place each of them in one of the four personality profiles. If they cross over between categories, place them in the one that is the closest.

3. Try to recall how you've interacted with each of them in the past.

4. Knowing the type of personality traits they exhibit, write down some ideas of how you think you could improve your working relationship by relating to them on their level.

Chapter 24

Postcards Get More Customers

Most mail advertising ends in the trash. But a postcard with the right message can increase your readership dramatically. Here are several examples of low-cost, high-impact mailing campaigns:

- While in Las Vegas for an annual quick printer's convention, the owner of a print shop in Solon, Ohio, bought 400 postcards from the MGM Grand. She brought them back home and had her kids hand address them to 400 businesses that were *not* her customers. The message on the postcard read, "Don't gamble with your printing needs. Bring this postcard in for a 10-percent savings on your first printing order." She received 100 redemptions! That's a 25-percent return. The reason? It didn't look like junk mail. If your prospects were to receive postcards from Vegas, they would probably ask themselves, "Who do I know there and how much did they win?" They'd then turn the card over to see who it was from. The message, such as the one the printer used, would get their attention and they would remember the offer. Plus, you mailed the cards for 20¢ each versus 32¢, which saves you postage.

- While we were in Nashville addressing a group of real estate agents from all over the United States, we told this story and then suggested that everyone find picture postcards, get a list of 25 potential clients, create a headline that tied into the picture on the postcard, and mail the cards from Nashville. One creative group found postcards with horses running through a pasture. Their headline: "Don't horse around when you want to sell your home fast."

- My favorite type of postcard mailer was done by a Realtor in Columbus. This real estate agent mailed a simple postcard to several hundred homes. He was offering a free home warranty to anyone who listed with him. But the postcard was boring. It was in black ink on grey cardstock and didn't look particularly appealing. As expected, 100 percent of his mailing was trashed. A week later, those same homes received an envelope from the same guy. Inside the envelope was the same postcard that had been crumpled up and then flattened. Attached to the crumpled postcard was a yellow sticky note that read, "Please don't throw this out again! This is important."

  People must have been saying to themselves, "Is this guy going through the trash? He must really know the neighborhood. We gotta give him a call!"

- Another clever use of an inexpensive postcard mailing was done by a scuba store owner in San Francisco who had planned a diving trip to Maui. Many of his customers inquired about the trip, but only a third actually signed up for it. The store owner kept the list of the people who couldn't make it. From Maui, he mailed picture postcards with a brief message about what a wonderful time they were having. What a great way to build up strong interest for future trips! Also, while he was there, he gave each of his participants three postcards with postage and asked them to write a "wish you were here" message to their scuba friends back home. It was a great way to generate referral business. That's how a Smart Marketer runs a business!

Smart Marketing action plan

1. Next time you attend a convention or conference, bring a mailing list of 25 potential clients with you.

2. Buy 25 picture postcards that represent the place you're visiting. Usually you can get a good deal on the ones from the hotel where you're staying.

3. Think of a clever headline to tie into the picture on the postcards.

4. Write a brief message telling your prospects that you're attending this event to learn how to better serve them and that you'll be in touch with them upon your return.

5. Mail the postcards at the postcard rate.

6. Upon your return, start your follow-up phone calls.

Chapter 25

Asking Questions Can Improve Sales

The secret to persuasive communication is this:

The person asking the questions controls the conversation.

There are several reasons for this. First, when you are asking a question, it forces the other person to pay attention to you. If you merely talk, the listener's mind can wander and think about other things. But the minute you say, "Let me ask you this...," the listener must pay attention because a response will be required. It is an automatic reflex.

Also, when you ask a question, you show compassion and concern for the needs of the prospective client. It helps you build rapport.

Perhaps the most important aspect of asking questions is that it allows you to gather valuable information from prospects. As you ask questions, you discover the needs and wants of your prospects. People love to talk about themselves, so let them, and in the process, your prospects disclose the information you need to help you sell.

Information-gathering is the secret. The more you know, the better off you are. And you can find all you need to know by simply asking and listening.

This means that you not only have to ask questions, but you have to ask the right kind of questions. There are two types of questions. A *closed-ended question* requires a yes or no response. The more pertinent is the *open-ended question,* which gets the prospect to provide you with information. The open-ended question usually begins with *what, why, where, when,* or *how.* You continue the probing by urging the client to give you additional information about a subject. You do this by simply asking him or her to continue.

- "That's interesting, tell me more."
- "Why do you say that?"
- "I see. Go on."
- "Why is that important to you?"

In order for you to stay in control of the selling process, when a prospect asks you a question, follow up with one of your own. This is usually when he or she is looking for emotional support. The person might say something like, "Do you think that's fair?" To which you respond, "What do you think?" or "How fair do you think it is?"

Solve their problems and they buy

People do not buy products and services, but rather, they buy solutions to problems. As a professional you want to help fill your customers' needs. You need to function as a problem solver for your clients. When they have objections, they put up barriers that you must begin to break down so that you can help them solve their problems.

So, to get your customer or client to give you the order or the commitment, you must first ask questions to find out needs, wants, and problems. Then you can offer your solutions, and you and your client can both be winners.

Smart Marketing action plan

1. Practice asking open-ended questions with a friend or family member, using the words *what, why, where, when,* and *how.*

2. Play the Hot Potato game. This is where you follow up a question with the answer and another question. For example, "Do you like movies?" "I love movies. What is your favorite movie?" The first person who does not ask a question loses.

3. Write down five open-ended questions you can use to sell a prospect.

4. Listen carefully to your prospect when you ask the questions, so you can learn about his or her problems. Then you can become the problem solver and get the sale.

Chapter 26

Help a Worthy Cause *and* Your Bottom Line

Raising money for a worthy cause might just be the perfect opportunity for your business to build sales. Such was the case when Dirk Todd, the golf pro at Raccoon International in Granville, Ohio, discovered that someone he knew needed a life-saving kidney transplant. While much of the cost of the operation was covered by insurance and grants, the organ rejection medication needed was not covered. With the help of the family and their friends, Dirk coordinated a benefit day at Raccoon International golf course. Money was raised in many different ways:

- Fees for rounds of golf.
- Fees for "gimmies," "pro shots," and "Mulligans."
- Food and beverage sales.
- Silent auction.
- Hole sponsorships.

Many area businesses donated food, so that 100 percent of the sales went to the cause. Donated food items included hamburgers, bratwursts, and a six-foot sub from Subway. One of the biggest moneymakers came from

Hosters, a local microbrewery, which donated kegs of its own beer for the event.

Dirk organized tee off times in the morning and afternoon to accommodate all the golfers. Eighteen local businesses sponsored individual holes, and the signs for those holes were donated by a local sign company. One very creative fund-raising element came from the sale of "gimmies," "pro shots," and "Mulligans." Gimmie ("give me") sales were by the foot. Prior to the event, lengths of string were sold for a buck a foot. Then, on a given green, the owner cashed in his or her string. If the string owner's ball landed within the length of the string, that was his or her final shot on that hole. On the eighth hole, a particularly rough hole that required golfers to drive over water, a player could make a donation to have a pro drive the ball for him or her. Players could also buy Mulligans, shots that were taken over without a penalty. These little games raised money and made the event more fun.

More than $5,000 was raised for the cause. After all of this work, what was the benefit to Dirk and Raccoon International? It brought many golfers out to his course who played it for the first time. As a result of that effort, many of them have become regulars and have brought other friends with them. This event was just one of several different marketing efforts Dirk used to create the best year in the history of the course.

Smart Marketing action plan

1. Find an individual or local organization that needs to raise money for a worthy cause.

2. Organize a special event, using your business as the focal point, to help raise money for the cause.

3. Structure the event so that money is raised when people are paying for your products or services. All profits should go to the cause.

4. At your event, offer "bounce back" certificates to participants to motivate them to, once again, visit your business. However, instead of a discount, the dollar amount on the certificate is to be donated to the cause. Use a tight expiration period (30 days, for example).

5. Promote the event through press releases, fliers, signs, banners, and other inexpensive means.

Chapter 27

Sell It With Seminars

The advantages of using the seminar as a marketing and sales tool, according to Michael Aun, coauthor of *The Toastmasters International Guide to Successful Speaking,* are:

- It puts you in front of potential clients.
- It gives you credibility.
- It positions you as an expert.
- It's free.

When Dr. Gary Berebitsky was just starting his pediatrics practice after finishing his residency in Phoenix, he used free seminars to help his practice through its infancy. His hospital sponsored prenatal care seminars for expectant mothers and he taught those seminars for free. It was a great public service for the hospital and Dr. Berebitsky, who both acquired new patients because of the combined effort.

Frank Foster, a patent attorney, was asked to speak at the Ohio Speaker's Forum. This is a group of professional speakers who also write and produce original material. One of their biggest concerns is protecting intellectual properties. Mr. Foster's seminar was an excellent way to attract potential clients who may need legal work done in this area.

Here are some steps you should take in planning your seminar:

Find a target audience. Mr. Aun suggests that you first identify your ideal target audience. What type of customers or clients do you want to attract?

Look for people magnets. Once you've determined the type of target audience you want, identify what they have in common and look for groups that have meetings these potential prospects attend.

Outline. Next, you need to figure out what you want to say. It's important to give your audience valuable information they can use, but not to give away the store at the same time. You also must not be a constant commercial. Depending on the amount of time you have, you need to figure out what you want to accomplish in this presentation. What are the main points you wish to make?

Practice. Find a no-liability group on whom you can practice. This practice group ideally should have no one in the audience that you would normally go after as a client. Use this group to work out the bugs in your presentation and the butterflies in your stomach. Don't expect to give a polished presentation immediately. That's okay. That's part of the process. Another good way to improve your presentation skills is to join a local Toastmaster's club.

Prepare handouts. With every presentation, prepare a leave-behind piece that your prospects can take home with them. It can be a combination of bullet points, fill-in-the-blanks, and illustrations if appropriate. Also, make sure that your name, business, address, and phone number appear at the top or bottom of every sheet of your handout. Make it easy for people to get in touch with you later.

Smart Marketing action plan

1. Identify the target group to which you want to present this seminar.

2. Identify organizations that have meetings that reach that target group.

3. Contact the group and offer to provide a free seminar.

4. Outline a one- to two-hour seminar that educates people about your product or service.

5. Practice your seminar with several groups of people that typically don't buy from you.

6. Join your local Toastmaster's club to help learn presentation skills.

7. Develop an audience handout, based on the seminar outline.

Chapter 28

Telemarketing for Telemarketers

One of the biggest challenges you'll have in building an effective telephone selling force is finding quality people who can actually sell your company's product or services over the phone. *Sell,* in this instance, can mean setting up good qualified appointments or actually closing the sale and taking the order. Here's a telemarketer's recruiting technique suggested to us by our good friend, George Walther, author of *Phone Power* and *Upside Down Marketing.* He suggested that in our regular classified advertising, we ask applicants to call our telephone number for details. We set up a separate phone line that is not part of our rollover lines. (When we're not recruiting, we use this line for outbound telephone activity.) The candidates call that number and reach our voice mail with an outbound message.

Sample script

"If you're looking for a sales position with un-limited potential, you've dialed the right number. This is Jeff Slutsky, president of Street Fighter Marketing, and in the next five minutes, I'll give you a detailed description of the telephone sales positions we have available. Toward the end of this message you will hear our complete compensation

....

package, including the hourly wages, bonus program, commission structure, and other special perks we offer. You'll be getting a lot of information, so feel free to call this number back as often as you like. You might even want to take some notes. Then, if you like what you hear, call back one more time and leave us a detailed audio resume right here on our machine. Now keep in mind: We are offering a telephone *sales* position, so *sell* us on why we should call you back for an interview...."

At that point, candidates start hearing details about the position. The neat thing about this approach is that you're not flooded with useless resumes; it's practically impossible to tell if someone can sell based on a piece of paper. Only those who are reasonably serious will bother to leave you a message. Of those, only a fraction will be worth following up on, based on their responses. Remember, you're concerned only with their selling skills over the phone. You don't care how they look or dress or who they know. If they communicate clearly with a strong selling message on why they're worth interviewing, you have good candidates.

The first interview

Once you have a strong "audio resume," conduct your first interview over the phone, too. Then, if that goes well, bring the candidate in for an in-person interview. Of course, its a good idea to run any recruiting practice by a labor attorney to make sure you're in compliance with all state and federal laws.

Smart Marketing action plan

1. Put a separate line into your phone system with its own number.

2. Write a script that explains the details of the position. Put the compensation toward the end of the script. Be sure to invite candidates to call back often, take notes, and create "audio resumes."

3. Record your outbound message. Do it until it's right.

4. Place your classified ad. Include only your special phone number for contacting you— no addresses.

5. With strong candidates, conduct your first interviews by phone.

6. If the interviews go well, conduct second interviews at your office.

Chapter 29

Clients Love You?
Get It in Writing!

One of the most powerful sales tools you can use is a client testimonial letter telling your prospect how wonderful you are. And the best part is, they cost you nothing to get! They can be used in several ways, including:

- In a promotional folder, mailed before a sales call.

- As part of a leave-behind piece after a sales call.

- As excerpts for your brochures and letters.

- As part of your "portfolio" when making a client presentation.

- Displayed in your office or store for customers to see.

Testimonial letters help your prospects feel more comfortable buying from you, because they add credibility to your message.

Ask immediately

The best time to get a letter is right after you've completed a good job for a client. Simply say, "You know, I'm very happy that you are pleased with our product (or service). It would really be helpful to me if you could send me a brief letter, on your letterhead, with a few of words about how we were able to satisfy your needs." Most clients are more than happy to accommodate you.

However, while most clients will agree to write you a letter, in reality, only a few get around to doing it. It's not a high priority for them. If you don't get a letter in a reasonable time, you might try calling back. Tell them that you realize they're very busy, and offer to write the letter for them. They can make changes if necessary and have it typed on their letterhead. Better yet, suggest that they send you several pieces of their stationery, and you'll have it typed up for them and mailed back for approval and signature. They can send it back to you in the enclosed self-addressed, stamped envelope. Some of the best testimonial letters we got...we wrote!

Cross-reference by industry and objection

Getting testimonial letters should become a regular part of your marketing and sales effort. The more you collect, the more ammunition you have. It's also a good idea to cross-index your letters by type of client and, perhaps, even by objection. For example, if you're talking to a new potential client and their concern is whether or not you can meet their deadline, you have 10 letters from previous clients that mention what a great job you did in meeting their difficult deadlines. These letters help enhance your credibility in the eyes of your prospect.

Smart Marketing action plan

1. Make a list of 25 satisfied clients.

2. Call them and ask for input on how you serviced their needs and for suggestions to improve it.

3. Assuming they were pleased, ask for a testimonial letter.

4. If you don't get it in a couple of weeks, call back and offer to write a "rough draft," because you "know they're busy."

5. As you collect the letters, start incorporating them into your sales and marketing process.

6. Repeat steps 1 through 5.

Chapter 30

Voice Mail Messages That Get Returned

Voice mail can be very frustrating for salespeople, because it makes it almost impossible to get through to your prospect. However, according to Orval Ray Wilson, coauthor of *Guerrilla TeleSelling,* there are some creative ways you can entice your prospect to return your voice mail message. We find that when we leave a standard message on voice mail, we'll get only half of our messages returned.

- **The insomnia message.** Because most voice mail has a time stamp, you can leave messages at odd hours to make a strong impression. "Hi, it's Mitchell Austin calling. It's 3:30 a.m., and I was just thinking about your account with us. I couldn't sleep, so I decided to leave you this message...."

- **The mile-high message.** Next time you're on a plane, use the onboard phone to call people you wish to reach. "Hi, it's Amanda Justin. I'm calling from 37,000 feet up on my way to Chicago. I was thinking about you and just had to call." According to Orval Ray, it's well worth the high price to leave an impression. If the person you're trying to reach is in the office, tell the secretary that you're calling *from the plane*, and you'll probably be put right through.

- **The stockholder's message.** Buy a few shares of your prospect's stock. Then leave a message introducing yourself as a concerned stockholder.

- **The "Who you're not" message.** "Hi. I'm *not* with the IRS, I'm *not* selling insurance, I'm *not* looking for a job or donation, I *don't* want to borrow money, but I *do* want to talk to you about..."

- **The "Disregard that message" message.** The first message you leave is, "Hi Char. Please disregard that last message. If you need anything else, please call me at..." Last message? What last message?

- **The "File a missing person report" message.** "Hello Ron. Your staff doesn't seem to know where you are, and frankly I'm concerned. I just wanted to let you know that I've filed a missing person report."

- **The persistent or pest message.** Larry Winget, a motivational speaker based out of Tulsa, Oklahoma, uses this one: "There's a fine line between being persistent and being a pest. I want to serve you well, yet never be a pest. Will you please call and tell me how best to serve you?"

- **The kiddy call message.** Have your kids make a call. "My daddy is going crazy waiting for you to call him back. Would you please call? As soon as you do, he can take me for ice cream."

Smart Marketing action plan

1. This week, each time you get someone's voice mail, try a different message from this chapter.

2. Be sure to write down which message you left for each voice mail contact.

3. Track the number of returned phone calls you get for each type of message you left.

4. Once you start to see a particular message working, start using it more often (with different clients, of course).

5. When you think of your own creative message, give it a try and track the results.

6. Caution: There's a fine line between *creativity* and *deception*. Don't risk making your prospect angry. Use some common sense.

Chapter 31

Web Site Savvy

If you have a Web site, or if you're thinking of having one created for you, there are several ideas you can use to help you get the most out of your online effort. According to Gary Coolidge of Coolidge Computers, a Web site-designing company in Powell, Ohio, "Once someone enters your Web site address, you want to make it easy for them to access that site and then to contact your company."

In-your-face phone and fax

Coolidge suggests that you use a "banner bar," which remains on the screen at all times. This is generally a strip across the top or bottom that contains one line of important information, such as your phone number, fax, e-mail address, etc. In this way, no matter where the viewer is in your Web site, your key contact information is always right in front of them.

Get down downloading

Speed of access is another critical element. If you keep people waiting too long to access your home page, they'll get impatient and might cancel the request. Keep your home page (the first page that appears when your Web site is accessed) simple. Save sound and video for your additional pages. Make sure your Web page designer uses the newest languages and technologies to insure the fastest download time possible.

Search engine shrewdness

When prospects search, you want to make it easy for them to find you according to subject or company name. There are generally two ways search engines select Web sites. The first is to scan your home page for keywords. The second is to look for "hidden keywords" that are imbedded in your Web site but don't show up on the screen. For example, many of our potential clients interchangeably use the terms "Street Fighter Marketing" and "Guerrilla Marketing" (the latter is our good friend Jay Conrad Levinson's term). So, on our home page, we have body copy that includes, "Guerrilla-style tactics." So, if someone is doing a search for "Guerrilla," we have a decent chance of getting selected as one possible site they should check out.

Typical typos

You might also want to include, with your hidden keywords, the different spelling possibilities in case your surfer doesn't spell that keyword the way you do. For example, we have "Street Fighter" on our home page, but we also have, as hidden keywords, "Streetfighter" (one word), "Street Fight," "Street Smart," "Street Wise," and "Street Marketing." These are all the different ways we've seen people mess up our company name over the years. We've also had to include 15 different spellings for "Slutsky," and believe it or not, "Street Walker Marketing."

To see how this looks, log onto our Web site at www.streetfighter.com.

Smart Marketing action plan

1. Use a banner bar that always has your phone number and/or e-mail address on-screen.

2. Keep your home page simple to maximize the speed that it downloads. Save the fancier stuff for later pages deeper into your Web site.

3. Have your site written in the most current language to improve download speed.

4. Make a list of keywords that potential clients may use in their searches. Include any common misspellings, as well. Those that aren't on your home page, use as hidden keywords or "meta tags."

5. Tip: List all of your *competitors* in the meta tags.

Chapter 32

Inviting New Sales

If you want people to open your promotional mailing piece, consider sending it in a format that almost always gets opened: an invitation. Getting your piece of mail opened and looked at is half the battle, so if you make yours look like a wedding invitation, for example, your readership will go up dramatically. Tie the headline of your offer into the invitation theme: *"We Invite You to Save Money"* or *"You're Cordially Invited to Our Sales Event."*

To make a full impact with your invitation mailer, use the following guidelines:

- It is expensive to use an actual wedding invitation, but you can achieve a similar impression by printing your piece on inexpensive textured paper, vertical format, 5½ x 8½, folded over to 5½ x 4¼. That size is printed two to a sheet of paper (or "two-up"), so to print 1,000, you need only 500 sheets, cut in half. Your quick printer will have matching envelopes. (This size is referred to as A-2 or Baronial.) If you use a larger size, it will cost you more. Use a script type style, but not one so fancy that it's difficult to read. You can use raised print if you like, but offset printing is less expensive and is printed on the premises. There are also wedding invitation kits you can buy for your computer that let you print short runs. In quantities of 25, they'll cost you about $1 each.

Occasionally, your quick printer or wedding invitation marketer may have a wedding invitation style that's discontinued or dramatically reduced in price for one reason or another. It's a long shot, but worth checking out. Compare the cost of a real invitation with that of creating your own "mock" invitation. If they're close and the style is impressive, you may consider it. Of course you won't need the return envelopes and extra inserts.

- Print the return address on the envelope flap—*but not your company name*—using a script typeface.

- Hand address the envelopes. If you use a printed label, you'll lose impact. It doesn't have to be calligraphy, but that would make even more of an impact. You can probably find someone to do this for you. Also, there are computer programs that can imitate your own handwriting.

- Don't use a bulk permit number or a postage meter. For maximum impact, mail it first class with a "Love" stamp. (Love stamps are usually used for wedding invitations.)

Smart Marketing action plan

1. Create a mailing piece that resembles a wedding invitation.

2. Handwrite the mailing address.

3. Use a script typeface for your return address, but don't use a company name.

4. Use a "Love" stamp, instead of a postage meter.

5. Your "invitation" should invite people to save money or discover what you have to offer. Create a theme.

Chapter 33

Recruiting: Alternatives to the Obvious

One of the biggest challenges among businesses is where to find qualified entry-level employees. Recruiting the right employee requires looking at alternate sources that could end up being the best. According to Bob Losyk, president of Innovative Training Solutions, Inc., of Davie, Florida, one very effective way to find an employee is to contact your local church group. By having churches advertise your opening through their bulletin boards, you have the ability to reach a very large group of potential employees at no cost to you. This is an excellent way to look for many entry-level workers. Other areas through the church include youth counselors and youth groups.

Bob also suggests using a variety of periodicals to get the word out about available job openings. The cost is very reasonable and you can target a specific industry, if need be. Just a few of those ideas include:

• Trade publications.

• Chamber directories.

• Community papers.

- Church/synagogue bulletins.
- Company newsletters.
- Ethnic publications.

Local groups and associations are also good ways to look for employees. Just a sample includes social clubs, senior/retirement centers, homeowner/condominium associations, YMCAs/YWCAs, fraternities/sororities, and bowling leagues.

Getting involved in your local community creates awareness about your company and about the kind of employees you are looking for, and it promotes good will. Many high schools have career days and are looking for guest speakers. Having your company represented at such events lets many potential candidates know about your company. This is a great way to get to know the high school counselor who would be a great referral resource.

If you are in the market for qualified individuals, the local newspaper is full of information on companies downsizing and going through layoffs, closings, and mergers. By being the first to contact those companies, you have the competitive edge to talk with the more qualified people. Bob also suggests advertising in the city of your biggest competitors. When Boeing Company of Seattle was in need of specialized employees, it advertised in the city where its biggest competitor, Airbus, was headquartered. Because of this strategy, Boeing hired many of Airbus's qualified workers.

It is also important not to overlook the Internet, which has become a great resource for job seekers. Your Web page is another way to promote your job openings, as well as linking to noncompetitive business Web sites.

Smart Marketing action plan

1. Identify the kind of employees you want, such as entry level or experienced.

2. Find periodicals where you think potential employees would look for work, and advertise in those.

3. Contact local churches to advertise about your openings on their bulletin boards or in their bulletins.

4. Look into using the Internet as a means to promote your job openings.

5. Have your current employees find you other qualified people and pay them a bonus for helping you.

6. Advertising on cable TV's bulletin boards allows you a cost-effective way to get the word out.

Chapter 34

Your Sense of Humor Improves Productivity

Humor can help you increase your creativity and productivity in the workplace, according to Steve Rizzo, a New York-based, highly sought-after corporate keynote speaker, consultant, and stand-up comic. Steve teaches how to effectively deal with stress and make smart decisions using his "Seven Attitudes of Humor." Steve told us that each attitude shows that a sense of humor is more than just one's ability to laugh. It's a unique state of mind, or a positive attitude that one has toward dealing with adversities.

Your sense of humor is your sense of perspective. It's a choice you have on how to deal with the stress and challenges you are confronted with each day. Problems arise because many people don't realize they have a choice. They feel stuck, cheated, lost, and victimized. It seems everyone else has what you want. You become overwhelmed. You say "what's the use," give up, and accept all the garbage that life throws at you every day, never knowing that you have the power to take control whenever you want.

New business sales calls are typical situations where this principle applies. Steve recalled being 45 minutes away from a very important audition. It was 98 degrees, the air conditioning wasn't working in the car, and he was stuck in the world's biggest traffic jam. He drove up to the toll booth and then realized that he had left his money at home. For some reason, he just looked at the attendant and said, "I'll have a couple of burgers, two fries, and get something for yourself, there, Sparky." He looked at Steve and said very seriously, "We don't have food here." Steve immediately responded nervously, "Then you'd better get some. You're holding up traffic."

Then they both started to laugh hysterically. All of the drivers in back of him were honking their horns and screaming, "Come on, we gotta get movin'." The attendant stuck his head out of the booth and waved Steve on, saying, "We ran out of food, try the next booth!" The coolest thing was that he let Steve go without paying, saying, "This toll's on me. I really needed to laugh today."

As a result, he went to that audition with a very positive attitude. He did so well that he got one of the most important breaks of his comedy career: his own Showtime special. Steve still wonders what would have happened if he had gone into the audition in the mood he was in before the toll booth incident.

Smart Marketing action plan

Your sense of humor is...

1. Your sense of perspective. It's a choice you have on how to deal with the challenges.

2. A constant smile from within that lets you know that you're okay and in control.

3. Knowing there is a brighter alternative to a potentially negative situation.

4. The ability to move forward with your life, in spite of what has happened to you in the past.

5. The ability to embrace change, and knowing with every door that closes in your life, there is an open window with a light shining through.

6. The ability to be happy and to enjoy yourself, in spite of it all.

7. The ability to laugh off your fears.

Chapter 35

Eight Secrets of Selling—Fast

An effective salesperson gathers the information neces-sary from the customer to make that sale, according to Harry Friedman of the Friedman Group in Culver City, California. Harry is the author of *No Thanks, I'm Just Looking* and editor of the retail newsletter *On the Floor*. He told us that there are eight key points that allow you to sell more effec-tively and in less time.

1. Concentrate on what your customer is saying. There are many distractions when talking to a potential customer. Try to tune into what the customer is telling you and block out everything else.

2. Establish eye contact. Maintaining eye contact enables you to understand things your cus-tomer's words alone may not be expressing. It also allows your customer to stay "locked in" on your presentation.

3. Listen to your customer's ideas—not just his or her words. Often your customer may not express him- or herself easily. By carefully listening, you can determine what your customer means and serve him or her without "being right" and los-ing the sale.

4. Don't jump to conclusions. Before you make a decision, it is important to listen to what your customer is saying. Don't make a decision on *a portion* of what the customer has said or you will miss out on useful information.

5. Never prequalify customers. If you judge a customer as unlikely to buy because of appearance or other factors, you're cheating yourself out of potential business. Treat everybody as a potential customer.

   At one of our seminars, Tony Crusco of Allied Bakers told me that he was at an industry trade show and went up to two shabbily dressed, unkempt youngsters, joked with them, and gave them each a toy (he did this with many youngsters at the trade show). Later, the lads' father approached him and thanked him for being so kind to his children. During the conversation, Tony found out that the father was a buyer for Kmart, and he eventually became Tony's largest bread account.

6. You should be *empathetic* with your customer, not *sympathetic*. Empathy is knowing how a person feels. Sympathy is feeling sorry for how that person feels. Don't trap yourself into "buying into" your customer's excuses for not buying.

7. One of the easiest ways to gain trust is to let the customer do the talking. Remember, you know what you know, but you don't know what the customer knows.

8. Use words to express, not impress. Keep your language simple and understandable. You are there to listen to your customer and give whatever information is necessary for him or her to decide to buy from you. Communication is a two-way exchange of ideas and concepts. A breakdown in the communication cycle results in a frustrated customer and a broke salesperson.

Smart Marketing action plan

1. Concentrate on what your customer is saying and listen to his or her ideas.

2. Don't make assumptions based on a portion of what the customer has said to you.

3. Don't prejudge whether a prospect will buy from you based on appearance or other factors.

4. Be empathetic, not sympathetic.

5. Make sure you let the customer do the talking.

6. Keep your language simple and understandable.

7. For a free copy of Harry Friedman's newsletter, *On the Floor*, call 800-544-9030.

Chapter 36

More Voice Mail Volleys

With increasing frequency, decision-makers are using voice mail instead of secretaries to screen calls and take messages. It's an alarming trend to many businesspeople. Kay Peterson, a Daytona Beach, Florida-based consultant, has a unique approach to the voice mail messages she leaves. Her company publishes a free newsletter for her clients and prospective clients. The newsletter provides valuable information, and her readers are always anxious to receive it. Therefore, she uses this newsletter as leverage with voice mail. If she does not get a returned phone call in a reasonable time, she leaves another message:

> "Mr. Smith, this is Kay Peterson. I left several messages with no response. Because I have not heard from you, I can only guess that you are no longer interested in what our company has to offer. I assume that our newsletter would be of no interest to you, either, so I'm going to remove you from the mailing list unless I hear from you shortly."

Usually within a matter of days, Ms. Peterson will get a return phone call.

Even if you don't have a newsletter, there are other ways to improve your chances of getting a return phone call.

- Be sure to leave your name and phone number. You'd be surprised how many people forget.

- Speak slowly and repeat your name and phone number during the message. After a while, your name is going to sound familiar and you'll have a better chance of a return phone call.

- Most prospects appreciate a salesperson's persistence in trying to reach them. So don't give up after a couple of calls—stick with it. However, there is a fine line between being persistent and being obnoxious.

- If you have out-of-town clients and you have an 800 or 888 number, leave it so the return call is not costing them anything.

There are times when you just want a yes or no answer, and the only nonacceptable answer is *maybe*. So, let prospects know if they don't want to talk with you to call after hours and leave a message on your voice mail.

Smart Marketing action plan

1. Use your newsletter or another value as an incentive to get a return phone call.

2. Always leave your name and phone number when you get someone's voice mail.

3. When you leave your name and number, speak slowly and repeat the information.

4. Make it easy for your client to get back to you by leaving your toll-free number.

5. Be persistent with your calling efforts, because persistence pays off.

Chapter 37

Scoring Points With Your Boss

Scoring points with your boss has always been necessary in the workplace, according to Cleveland-based Alan R. Schonberg, co-author of *169 Ways to Score Points With Your Boss* (co-written with Robert L. Shook). Alan is the CEO of Management Recruiters International (MRI), the world's largest search firm. Jerry Harris, one of three general managers of Management Recruiters of Columbus, told us, "Over your career you'll probably work for several different companies and odds are high you'll always have a boss." Here are some of their favorite point makers:

Read your company's annual report. It contains a wealth of information and you can score points by quoting obscure bits of information your boss might have skipped.

Make your customers rave about you. Customer loyalty results in referrals and repeat business, so bosses love to hear customers rave about outstanding employees.

Never say anything negative about your former company or boss. If you criticize a former boss, your new boss may wonder what you're saying behind his or her back.

Get to the point. No doubt your boss is busy and even if you feel you don't get enough quality time with your boss, you may try to take advantage of that time. The more you drag out your point, the less valuable you become.

Never argue with your boss. You can't win. You can only end up getting your boss upset with you. Use a different tactic to get your point across.

Realize that the squeaky wheel does not always get the grease. To paraphrase a Japanese proverb, the nail that sticks up the highest gets pounded the hardest. Nobody likes a complainer. The constant grumbler is unlikely to become one of the boss's favorites.

Admit your mistakes. This is not a sign of weakness. On the contrary, it takes a strong person to admit a mistake. Good bosses understand this and know that competent people are capable of saying, "I was wrong." Risk-taking is necessary in the business world and mistakes are a part of it.

Be sure to attend your boss's big speech. Chances are your boss will appreciate a friendly face in the audience to offer support. After the speech, find something to sincerely praise about it.

Be coachable. This means taking orders. It also means being willing to learn and grow.

Smart Marketing action plan

1. Read your company's annual report.
2. Make your customers rave about you.
3. Don't bad-mouth a former boss.
4. Get to the point quickly.
5. Never argue with your boss.
6. Don't complain.
7. Admit your mistakes.
8. Attend your boss's big speech.
9. Be coachable.

Chapter 38

The Blow-out Promotion

If you want to get tons of customers to come to your business for the first time, try a "blow-out" event. The blow-out relies on a crazy price strategy. You lower the price so ridiculously low that customers can't afford to miss it. On the surface, a blow-out may appear to be a money loser. The lead item at these events, in fact, will lose money, but the goal is to get people in the front door.

Luby's Cafeteria in Tampa did a "Customer Appreciation Day" for its blow-out. The offer was half off everything for one day. A banjo player, a magician, and balloon artist made the event festive and kept the guests entertained while they waited to be seated. The interior of the restaurant was decorated to reinforce the festive spirit.

This kind of promotion is great, because you will get many new people to try your business. However, the key is to make sure that there is enough food to go around. If you upset your customers by not having enough product, then the event loses its benefit. Luby's management knew from experience that the guests would try the most expensive meals, so they stocked up on all the fish and meats.

Not only do you need to have enough product, you also need to make sure you have enough labor. Luby's decided that this promotion was so important, they had all the other Luby's general managers in the area there to lend a helping hand. This proved to be a great asset, because when the cafeteria was packed and everybody was under a great deal of pressure to perform, they had experienced staff.

The result of Luby's event was dramatic. Sales tripled for the day and customer counts quadrupled. The important factor was that sales were up for the month by 13 percent following the promotion. The manager guessed that at least half of the people coming to this event were new faces.

It's a good idea to offer a "bounce-back" certificate. This gives all those new customers an opportunity to get a great value on their next visit. Coming back again soon, preferably within 30 days, is important to creating a more loyal customer base. It also gives those customers an opportunity to see your operation under more normal circumstances.

Smart Marketing action plan

1. Create a good reason to have a "blow-out" event for your business (for example, customer appreciation, anniversary, grand opening or reopening, etc.). Give yourself enough lead time to plan it right.

2. Take one of most popular items and price it ridiculously low (a large pizza for $1.99, movie rentals for 25¢, a full-service car wash for 99¢, hamburgers for 75¢, 25¢-a-gallon gas, an oil change for $3.99, etc.).

3. Only discount the main item. Keep all others regular price.

4. Do this for one day only and at one location only if you have multiple locations.

5. Load up on product and labor. Don't get caught short, or this event will do more harm than good.

6. Create a "bounce-back" certificate to bring customers back again. The offer should be a normal discount or value-added.

7. Promote your event four to seven days beforehand. Don't forget to invite your regular customers, too.

Chapter 39

Write the Book and You're the Expert

You can be perceived as the top expert in your field or your marketplace if you write and publish a book on the subject. Unfortunately, only a small number of books actually get published, according to Jeff Herman of the Jeff Herman Literary Agency in New York.

Jeff, who is the author of *Writer's Guide to Book Editors, Publishers, and Literary Agents*, suggests that if you're looking to use your book as a promotional tool, you should consider writing a self-published anthology. Here's how it works:

First, contact several professionals in the field that is related to, but not competitive with, yours. Three examples might include:

- Finance: CPA services, tax law, financial planning, mortgage brokering, banking, payroll service, etc.

- Office: Computer hardware/software/networking/ training, copiers, telecommunications equipment, long-distance and local phone services, office supplies, office equipment, insurance, etc.

- Home: Remodeling, spas and pools, landscaping, lawn service, roofing, painting, decorating, furniture, home entertainment and appliances, insurance, real estate, etc.

You'll need between 10 and 15 participants. Each "expert" writes a 2,000- to 3,000-word chapter for the book, which is printed in paperback. Every participant agrees to buy a minimum number of copies, let's say 1,000. The cover is customized for each participant, so that each person's picture and company is featured prominently on his or her copies. Each participant agrees to provide a copy of the book to their existing customers as a "thank you." You might want to compare your customer lists to avoid duplications. In this way, you distribute 1,000 books, but you're also getting exposed to 14,000 other potential new customers.

In these quantities, and after you account for initial setup costs, you can print the books for about $2 to $3 a piece. Give it a retail price of $20, even though you'll be giving them away. Also, when the publisher prints your version of your cover, you should consider getting a couple of thousand extra covers printed. Once it's on press, it only costs about 10¢ each to run the extras. Trim the backs and spines and you have a high-quality promotional piece that can also double as a postcard.

Your chapter should contain useful information. Don't overtly promote your company or services in the chapter. You can use success stories and a lot of "how to" information. If you publish a newsletter, you could use some of those articles as the basis for your chapter. You can also use information in your own trade journals, but be sure to quote your sources. If you can't write, hire a ghostwriter to do it for you.

Smart Marketing action plan

1. Contact 10 to 15 "complementary" businesspeople to contribute a chapter to an anthology book geared to your target customer base.

2. Write your chapter or hire a ghostwriter to do it for you. It should be 2,000 to 3,000 words, with useful information.

3. All participants have to agree to buy a certain number of copies.

4. Print covers so they're customized for each participant.

5. All participants should agree to distribute the books to their customers.

Chapter 40

Healthy Body, Healthy Business

More businesses are finding that it makes "bottom-line" sense to encourage employees to get and stay in shape. By having their employees eat healthy and exercise, it not only saves corporations millions through a reduction in insurance costs, but it also increases the employees' productivity. According to Doug Owens, a personal trainer in Worthington, Ohio, "Increasing the fitness of an employee through nutrition and exercise dramatically reduces sick time and reduces serious illnesses and injuries. Owens also says that when individuals participate in simple exercise programs, they experience a positive change in their overall outlook on life, therefore increasing their productivity.

Doug recommends a simple fitness program for busy businesspeople that improves health in four areas:

1. Nutrition.
2. Strength.
3. Flexibility.
4. Cardiovascular.

The following executive fitness program improves circulation, flexibility, and functional range. The exercises should be performed slowly and smoothly, starting with several repetitions and working up to 20 to 30. (Please consult a physician when starting any exercise program.)

Functional strength training

Push-ups and sit-ups are an easy way to begin to build strength. These are perfect for busy travelers, because they can be done in any hotel room. If the hotel has an exercise room, use light weights for arm curls and shoulder shrugs. Increase the weight after your strength increases.

Aerobic conditioning

First start off by walking to build endurance. Do this two to three times a week, and build from there. Once your endurance is up, you can start other aerobic exercises, such as jogging, bicycling, jazzercize, and other types of work-outs. Most hotels provide exercise facilities, such as stationary bikes, treadmills, and stair-stepping machines.

Flexibility and stretching exercise

Identify several areas that need stretching and begin to slowly stretch those areas. This should be done for your warm-up.

Stress management

Stress management is crucial to maintaining your health. Things you can do to help cope with stress include:

Breathing tactics. When exercising, breathe in through your nose and out your mouth. Try to get as much oxygen into your lungs as you can. This technique is also perfect for calming jittery nerves before a major meeting.

Improved sleeping habits. Sleep is very important to managing stess, and it can keep you from getting run down. Try to get at least eight hours a day. If you can't, then try to take a 20-minute nap during the day. By applying this simple suggestion, you will stay refreshed and your productivity will increase. Once you start your regular exercise program, you may find that you have an easier time falling asleep.

Smart Marketing action plan

1. Keep a log of everything you eat for one week.

2. Review your food log to determine where you can cut down on calories, especially those calories from fat.

3. Start with a simple exercise plan two to three times a week.

4. Balance your program with strength, flexibility, and cardiovascular exercises.

5. Consult your doctor before starting any program.

Chapter 41

The Virtual Office: Is It for You?

In today's modern business world, the virtual office allows you to use advanced technology to compete with the big boys and leave your competition in the dust. Gary Coolidge, executive vice president of Coolidge Computer Services in Powell, Ohio, says "The virtual office increases employee efficiency to improve customer service and reduce operating costs." According to Coolidge, the major advantages are:

- **Reduced overhead.** The virtual office gives you the freedom of not having to use expensive office space. As long as your business lets you visit clients at their locations, you can work right out of your home. By using voice mail, cellular phones, and a paging system, your support staff can dedicate their time to administrative responsibilities, instead of just answering the phones and taking messages. Office equipment is a major expense for any business owner, but with companies such as Kinkos to copy and print materials for you, you don't have to make that initial purchase or lease.

- **Increased freedom.** When you have an office, you feel obligated to spend time there. Where is your revenue generated? Is it in your office or in front of prospects and clients? The virtual office gives you the freedom to spend more time with your revenue generators (your clients).

- **Improved customer service.** With your virtual office, you can now provide your customers with a phone number that instantly contacts your pager or cellular phone. That will make it easier for your prospects and customers to reach you, increasing your value. Likewise, the Internet allows your customers to contact you 24 hours a day, using e-mail. It can be a real benefit to a customer knowing that they have access to you constantly. You can also use e-mail to contact your employees and vendors. Not only is this instantaneous, but it also cuts down on long-distance phone calls.

- **Increased business resources.** By using the World Wide Web, you can find current information about your industry or your customers instantly. There is also the advantage of having "millions" of prospects at your fingertips using the Internet. Prospects and customers can find you easily or communicate with you via a Web site.

The virtual office allows you to respond to a customer *now*! In this fast-paced world, your customers want information yesterday. If you are going to stay ahead of the game and compete with the big boys, the virtual office gives you complete freedom to achieve your business goals and objectives.

Smart Marketing action plan

1. Analyze how much office space you can reduce if you increase your ability to visit more prospects and clients on-site.

2. Use voice mail and a pager to free up your staff to do more administrative work.

3. Make it easy for your customers to contact you with a pager or cellular phone and make sure you respond quickly.

4. Use the World Wide Web to research your industry to know where the trends are going.

Chapter 42

More Advice on the Web

The Internet can bring you business if you know how to use it properly. By developing a Web site, you open the doors to a new and exciting way to promote your business. When developing your Web page, focus on and make available the products and services that best illustrate the strength of your company. This way, the consumer uses your Web site not only to learn about your business, but to actually order your products.

George Farris, president of Farris Advertising, says that there are many advantages of having a Web site.

- **Global awareness.** You have the potential to reach prospects all over the world. Marc recently did some work for a client in the Middle East, and during their initial conversation, the client requested information about our company, Street Fighter Marketing. The client was directed to our Web site, where he was able to get the information he needed right away.

- **They find you.** Your customers are looking for your information, and that is why they found you. When you get a response because of a Web site, it is easier to sell.

- **You're open 24 hours.** Your customers can order products and learn about your company and services anytime they want. You are marketing yourself without the increase in travel and salaries. Your Web site is a salesperson that never sleeps, eats, or goes on vacation.

- **Unlimited customers.** When you have a Web site developed, you are available to millions of "visitors."

- **It's easy to modify.** A Web site is easy to update if it is designed to be modular. You can add new products and services at very affordable rates.

- **You can customize.** Because users can "browse" certain sections of your Web site, you can customize your message to target certain groups, even in different languages.

Farris offers some tips in setting up and maintaining your Web site:

- **Use a professional.** Find a professional who specializes in developing Web sites. It can be very frustrating to your customers if your Web page takes too long to load or if it looks third rate. Remember, it is a one-time cost, but you will need to budget for regular maintenance and updates.

- **Promote the Web site.** If you use media to promote your business, mention your Web site. Put the address on all your printed materials, including envelopes, business cards, stationery, and labels.

- **Get them to come back.** It is important to give the consumers who visit your Web site a reason to come back again. The more they come back, the better chance you have to sell them.

Because the Internet provides your business with inexpensive space, interactive information, easy-to-update Web pages, and immediate response, the Web site can provide your business with a versatile sales and marketing tool.

Smart Marketing action plan

1. Use a professional to develop your Web page.

2. Your home page should load up quickly.

3. If you have a product, customers should be able to order online.

4. Promote your Web page through other media.

5. Include your Web page information on all your printed materials.

6. Give your customers a reason to visit you frequently.

Chapter 43

Getting Business from Trade Shows

Many people attend trade shows, but end up with little or no business. If you are going to attend a trade show, there are key points to remember to get business. According to Steve Miller, president of The Adventure of Trade Shows in Seattle, Washington, there are six elements in getting business from a trade show.

1. **List of prospects.** Before you go to the show, identify 20 to 30 prospects from your database and create a hit list. Do anything you can to see each one at the trade show. Steve desperately wanted to see a prospect at a show he was attending. After numerous phone calls with no response, he knew he had to try something completely different. Walking through the airport, he noticed a flight insurance machine and a light bulb went off. He purchased flight insurance, making the prospect the beneficiary, and sent it to him with a "just thinking of you" note. The prospect called Steve, agreed to meet with him at the show, and became one of his largest clients.

2. **Booth design.** Making your booth unique and different gets attention from prospects. Miller says, "Make your booth a *visual train wreck.*" For

example, a client on a low budget attended a confectionery trade show. His special item was a piece of candy in a gold wrapping. He covered his entire booth in black, from the background to the table, and dropped thousands of the candy in gold wrapping all over the table. The contrast in color between the black and gold made a major impact.

3. **The message.** The message displayed in your booth needs to be a benefit to your customers. Call 12 of your top customers and ask why they do business with you. Once you find a common response that is a benefit, use that as your message.

4. **Your people.** You and the people with you in your booth are the most important factor at your trade show. Make everyone look unique —with special ties, coats, or even flowers—so your customers can distinguish your company from everyone elses. Also, you and your people should talk to anyone who comes within 10 feet of your booth. Remember, you are there to get leads.

5. **An understanding.** After you talk with a prospect, make sure you both have an understanding of what the next action is going to be. Whether it's a phone call, a quote, literature, or even a face-to-face appointment, make sure both parties know exactly what's going to happen.

6. **Follow-up.** Extend the show by one day and do follow-up. More than 80 percent of the people who have booths at trade shows will do nothing or very little afterwards. At a trade show, it is not quantity that counts, but quality. If you can come away with a handful of good leads and then follow up, the chances of success increase dramatically.

Smart Marketing action plan

1. Make a list of 20 to 30 prospects to contact at the trade show.

2. Make sure your booth is unique and completely different from the rest.

3. Create a message to display in your booth that shows a benefit.

4. Make your people working the booth distinguishable to your customers.

5. Make a commitment to each prospect to do something.

6. Follow up and do it.

Chapter 44

Dealing With the Difficult Buyer

Salespeople have many different kinds of customers to sell. It is important to establish what kind of customers they are, so you know how to sell to them. Harry Friedman of the Friedman Group in Culver City, California, and the author of *No Thanks, I'm Just Looking,* divides the types of customers into several categories. Here are just a few:

- **The Marcel Marceau type.** This customer has a quiet personality and is shy to talk. As a salesperson, you have done everything properly, from opening the sale to probing, but have gotten little response from the customer. You asked questions about what the customer wanted and have received little or no information. What's a salesperson to do?

  Solution: One way to handle this type of customer is to go for the close. Trying to close the sale will initiate the customer to either buy or not buy. If the customer isn't ready to buy, then focus on asking open-ended questions to get some additional information. With this additional information, then go again for the close.

- **The Monty Hall type.** This customer wants "to make a deal" on everything. He or she wants to buy the finest merchandise for less than your cost and is very relentless in his or her pursuit to get it. The customer agrees on a price only after you offer 50 percent off another item. When you stand firm on your offer, this customer insists on free delivery. What's a salesperson to do?

Solution: Let this customer know that you have gone as low as you have the authority to go. However, you're willing to make a call, if he or she doesn't mind waiting, to the "boss" (even if you are the boss), who can approve a larger discount. Go in the back room and make the call. Go back to the customer and say, "I told the boss you were a good customer and I would like to do better for you, but after looking up the pricing, he told me I couldn't go less. I tried!" This customer now knows the bargaining days are over and it is time for you to close the sale.

- **The wishy-washy customer.** This one likes the product, can afford it, but just can't seem to say yes. Making decisions is very difficult for the wishy-washy type. Every time you spend time with this customer, he or she leaves without buying. What's a salesperson to do?

  Solution: This customer can't make up his or her mind, so it is up to you to help. Confirm the choice by commenting on what a wise selection the customer has made. Mention other satisfied customers who have made a similar purchase. To help with the buying decision, write up a sales slip or delivery order. The goal is to build up the customer's confidence and close the sale.

Smart Marketing action plan

1. Study the solutions to each category, so you know them well.

2. Role play the solutions with other employees until you feel comfortable.

3. Identify those customers who fall into a difficult category.

4. Try the solutions out on customers.

5. Modify the solutions, if need be.

Chapter 45

Rewarding Your Younger Work Force

Businesses today rely on younger workers to make up their work force. Rewarding these workers keeps them motivated and decreases the chance of them looking for other job opportunities. Training new employees is far more costly than rewarding a current staff and keeping them happy.

According to Bob Losyk, author of *Managing a Changing Workforce,* there are a variety of ways to reward young workers.

- Have an employee-of-the-week award, which is chosen by peers. This is an excellent way to see who the leaders are in your company and who has management potential.

- Have your employees select a person to receive the supervisor-of-the-month award. You not only reward the supervisor, but you find out who your employees like to work under.

- You can generate excitement and enthusiasm among your employees by creating outrageous awards, such as service maniac of the month, service rookie of the month, idea of the month, or even a spirit-of-the-company award.

Smart Marketing

- Highlight employees with photos on bulletin boards or display cases, or give them a special parking space for a period of time. This gives the owner or manager a double benefit. Not only do you recognize the employee for a job well-done, but other employees who want to receive the same honor will increase their productivity.

- Have the company owner or a top manager write a "job well-done" letter and mail it to the employee's home. Or put an employee's letter from a satisfied customer on the bulletin board.

- The company's owner or managers should praise or acknowledge employees periodically in front of peers to make them feel like part of the team.

- Give out little notes with positive comments. After an employee receives 10, he or she gets a prize, bonus, or extra time off.

- Reward your employees for service innovations, cost savings, and creativity.

- Have employees refer friends as candidates for employment. If a candidate meets certain standards of service within a certain time frame, the employee who referred him or her wins a prize.

- Pay for employees to attend seminars of their choice in related fields. Continuing education is an important motivator.

- For achieving superior levels of service, have your employees earn time-off credits.

- Have mystery shoppers award instant prizes to employees for giving superior service.

These are just some ideas you can use to reward your employees for exceptional work or service provided to your customers and clients. As the employer, you need to be consistent with your reward system, so your employees know what you expect from them and what they can expect in return.

Smart Marketing action plan

1. Identify one or two rewards that you can implement right away.

2. Set up the criteria for your employees to earn those rewards.

3. When a reward is earned, post it so that other employees know who is being recognized.

4. Every couple of months, change the reward system.

5. Ask your employees what kind of prizes they would like to get.

6. If you have any other reward programs that have been successful, we would like to hear about them.

Chapter 46

The Blitz Promotion

If customers won't come to you, perhaps you should go to your customers. That's what a neighborhood "blitz" program can do. You have a group of volunteers or employees canvass the neighborhood, distributing fliers, coupons, freebie cards, door hangers, or whatever you need to get people in the front door. Chick-fil-A, a successful fast-food chicken chain, uses free sandwich cards. The owners are more than willing to give away sandwiches, because they know that once customers try them, they'll have a lot of repeat business.

A bank got its neighboring branch managers together for a day. Because they weren't used to "cold calling," they visited the area businesses in groups of three. They introduced themselves, handed out cards, literature, and logo-clad glass jars filled with candy. Then they asked a few questions about each business's banking needs. Strong leads were followed up later by a branch manager.

To make marketing blitz efforts successful, follow these guidelines:

1. Assign a territory for each participant, so that there is no overlap. For sales-reluctant people, assign small groups.

2. Everyone should go out at the same time. If you split up, meet somewhere for lunch to review your progress and to fire each other up again.

3. Have specific printed pieces to distribute. Anything with a free trial will be more effective, because it gives prospects a reason to visit your business. Have plenty of business cards. Every person who runs or manages a business should have these.

4. When selling services, ask a few questions to uncover needs and potential future business.

5. Limit the time you spend out. A day or two is best, but no longer than a week. If you stretch it out too long, you'll begin to waste time. The tighter the timetable, the higher the energy.

6. Don't spend too much time with any one customer. If need be, make an appointment for a later time.

The reverse blitz

A college bookstore was able to get customers to come to *them*—and got the "jump" on its competition—by offering free bungee jumping with each textbook purchase. This turned what would normally be a simple sale into a major event. The cost was $5,000 for the bungee-jumping equipment, but it brought in more than $75,000 in sales. Students even went to the competitor's by mistake and asked if they were the ones doing the free bungee jumping.

Smart Marketing action plan

1. Organize a group of employees or volunteers and pick a day to canvass your neighborhood.

2. Assign specific territories to each participant.

3. Create a special value certificate or select a give-away item for distribution that promotes your business.

4. Give each participant a specific number of pieces or items to distribute.

5. For services, generate leads that can be followed up later.

Chapter 47

Sell the "End Result"

When you're introducing your product or service to a potential customer, you should capture his or her attention immediately. The best way to do that is to tell your prospect what the "end result" of having used your product or service will be. In our case, we would not say, "We conduct seminars, workshops, and consulting projects in local marketing and telephone sales." That gives our prospect just enough information to decide that there is no interest. Instead, we *would* say, "We can teach you how to advertise, promote, and increase sales without spending a lot of money." Instead of telling your prospect what you *do*, stress the unique *benefits* of your product or service.

One of the most challenging benefit statements we had to work on was for a life insurance agency. The minute someone says he or she sells life insurance, people head for the doors. It seems that nobody wants to talk to a life insurance salesperson. The challenge was to create a benefit statement that would grab a prospect's attention and avoid the turnoff associated with life insurance.

You can test the effectiveness of your benefit statement at a party. In a conversation, when someone asks what you do, presenting your benefit statement should cause the person to respond, "No kidding. How do you do that?" In essence, he or she is asking you for a sales pitch about your product or service.

In the case of the life insurance salesperson, one of his major areas of concentration was helping well-to-do people plan for significant retirement income. So, the benefit statement we developed was, "We specialize in helping people accumulate more than a million dollars for retirement, with only small monthly contributions." Nowhere did you hear the words "life insurance."

Ask yourself, "What do I do that clients will find very valuable?" How can you phrase it so that, when asked, most people will response, "No kidding. How do you do that?"

For example, if you said merely that you're an accountant or a CPA, that might be of some interest. On the other hand, if you said, "I specialize in helping people dramatically reduce their tax bill," that would get most people's attention. The fact that you're a CPA will come up later in the conversation. If you stress being a CPA, then you're automatically lumped in with all the other CPAs.

A stockbroker might say, "I specialize in finding undervalued companies with strong long-term potential for people who want to maximize their investment profits."

The branch manager of a local bank might say, "I specialize in helping businesses handle just about all their finance needs, including establishing lines of credit and cash flow management." He sells loans, CDs, and checking accounts, but that's irrelevant. What's important is the result, the benefit of using this banker's services.

Smart Marketing action plan

1. Write down all of the benefits or the end results a prospect can expect after using your product or service.

2. Create your own benefit statement using the following format: "I specialize in (benefit) without (negative)."

3. Practice using your benefit statement when you meet people. Work it into conversations and gauge their reaction to it.

4. Modify your benefit statement as needed for specific products and services or for different types of prospects.

Chapter 48

Inbound Telephone Opportunities

When customers call to inquire about your products or services, you have an opportunity to convert interest into sales if you know how to effectively handle those calls. If you don't take phone orders, don't settle for simply giving out prices, because once you give a price, there's a good chance you'll never see that prospect.

Often, people call and ask only about price. Many of them are letting their fingers do the walking and are trying to compare your prices with those of your competitors. However, if you were to only give a price, you would never know whether you had a shot at that business or not. You wouldn't even know if the price was a fair comparison when quality and service were considered. To handle this type of call, you need to gain control of the conversation by *asking* questions, rather than *answering* them. Be prepared to ask at least five basic *when*, *how*, and *what* questions. And when you do give a price, always follow up with a question, such as, "Is that in your budget?" If your price is too high, you may have other options to attract that caller.

Capture names and numbers

After you've asked your five basic questions and have given some information to your prospect, you should make sure to "capture" the name and phone number of the caller. This is then added to your database. Anyone who calls you, whether the person buys or not, is an important contact for future business. Caller ID can be useful for this, if it's available in your area.

Always be selling

Bill Ellis of E & E Remodelers in Columbus, Ohio, tells the story of how he got a big window replacement job because of a wrong number. He had just gotten home, beat after a tough day, when the phone rang. "Is Joe there?" the woman on the line asked. "There's no Joe here, but I'm a remodeler. Are you interested in some remodeling in your home?" he asked, without missing a beat. "As a matter of fact, we were just talking about replacing our windows." He went right over to her house and wound up with a big sale.

Marc uses a similar approach at our office. Whenever he gets telemarketing calls, he responds by letting them know that their telephone selling skills were okay, but that they could stand some improvement. Then he offers to sell them our audio album, *The 33 Secrets of Street Smart Tele-Selling* for $59.95. Most of the callers want to hang up in a hurry. To date, he's had one sale from someone who was telemarketing copy machines. She bought. We didn't.

Smart Marketing action plan

1. Create a list of five or six questions you can ask inbound callers. These questions usually revolve around *when*, *how*, and *what*.

2. When you finally give a price over the phone (*after* you've asked your basic questions), follow up with a question to get feedback.

3. If the price is all right, set up an appointment to bring the prospect in.

4. If the price is too high, ask more questions to find out what can be done to satisfy the prospect. Once you've done that, go back to step #3.

5. Capture names and numbers whenever possible for your database.

Chapter 49

How to Say No to Donation Requests

How do you handle requests for donations? If you gave money to every cause that came calling, you could easily go broke, yet you don't want to get a "bad guy" reputation in your community.

First, determine if the caller is a professional solicitor working in a "boiler-room operation" or a legitimate member of your local community. If it is a boiler-room operation, you can turn the person down without the fear of getting a less-than-positive image in the community. To determine if it is such an operation, one neat trick is to tell the caller that it sounds like a good deal, but you'll have to talk to your partner, supervisor, or whatever to get a decision. Ask for the organization's phone number, so you can call back.

If it's a boiler-room operation, the caller will say that he or she can't wait for a return call or that the organization is not equipped to handle incoming calls, so that you should wait until next year to donate.

One retailer has a unique way of dealing with these calls. When the solicitor asks, "How are you today?" He answers, "Lousy. Business is terrible, my wife just left me, my kids are dropping out of school, and then some idiot just called and tried to sell me some worthless ad in a worthless program. Now, how can I help you?" Usually about halfway through the recitation, he hears a click.

Many times, requests for donations or program advertising come from members of your community. You don't want to get a negative image in the community, so you have to be careful. The ideal way to handle these requests is to direct them to someone else—an advertising agency, home office, or an area supervisor. Tell callers that those decisions are made elsewhere, and give them the number. If you can give them a long-distance number, you'll get rid of half the requests right away. (Notice that you're not turning them down, someone else is.)

There may be times when you have to deal with requests yourself. Here is a way I've found to be very effective: First, listen to the caller's pitch all the way through. Then say, "Gee, that sounds like a worthwhile program, and I would really like to help you. But here is my problem: We set aside a budget at the beginning of our fiscal year for such worthy programs. Unfortunately, the budget is all used up this year. Perhaps if you could get to us earlier next year, we could help you out. Thanks for calling."

By "next year," committees change, people move, and when it is time for you to get your phone call from that group again, it will probably be a different person, so you can use the same excuse.

Smart Marketing action plan

1. Determine if a request for a donation is from a local member of your community or a professional solicitor.

2. If it is a professional solicitor, deny the request.

3. If it is a legitimate member of the community, say that the budget has been used up this year and to get in touch with you earlier next year.

Chapter 50

Marketing With Photographs

As a professional salesperson or executive, your photograph is a powerful marketing tool, according to Dawn Waldrop, president of Best Impressions. Your photograph has a variety of uses, including directories, press releases, ads, brochures, and fliers. Here are some tips to help you successfully market with photographs:

- Have a new photograph taken every two years or 10 pounds, whichever comes first.

- Use a black-and-white photo (4 x 5 works best).

- Have a hair stylist style your hair just before the photo shoot.

- Background color is critical. The best colors are a medium-soft gray or blue.

- Your body position also makes a difference. If you are a large person, you should turn your shoulders slightly toward the camera with your head tilted slightly to the side. If you are a small person, face toward the camera.

- We all have a best side. Make sure your best side faces the camera.

Smart Marketing

- A bust shot is the best for reprinting pictures in newspapers or magazines. You do not want your head to fill up the whole picture, as it would with a head shot, or your whole body looking too small, as it would with a full-body shot.

- Leaning forward toward the camera gives a friendly feeling. A straighter posture gives a stern impression. What message do you want to send?

- When viewing the proofs, make sure you are in the middle of the photograph.

- Let the photographer know that details are important to you. Ask him or her to make sure your clothes lay neat and smooth.

- Men, powder your face to take away any shine and to give a matte look. Camera lights create a shine on the skin. If you are bald or balding, powder your head.

- Women, powder your face after your makeup is complete. Put your makeup on twice and blend in between each application. Wear a brighter or darker lipstick than you normally would, otherwise you will look like you don't have any on.

- Men, wear a tie in a darker color than your shirt.

- Women, wear a blouse lighter than your jacket, if you are wearing a medium- to dark-color jacket.

- Darker jackets or outfits work best to create a contrast with the background color. Make sure your outfit contrasts with the background color.

- Long sleeves always look best, because they represent a high level of professionalism.

- If you wear glasses, avoid a reflection from camera lights. Verify this with the photographer before the session. If you normally wear glasses, wear them in the photo.

- Women, keep your jewelry simple and slightly larger, otherwise your accessories will not show in the picture.

- There shouldn't be any props in the background.

- Use simple patterns or prints.

Smart Marketing action plan

1. Have a professional photo taken every two years.

2. Use your photo for all press releases and promotional material.

3. Have your photo taken in color, but have both color and black and white available.

4. Make sure the shot you choose sends the appropriate message to the viewer.

Chapter 51

Common Sense Secrets for Selling

According to Hal Becker, Author of *Can I Have Five Minutes of Your Time?*, there are some "Common Sense Secrets" for selling more. Here are four of his favorites:

Common Sense Secret #1. Send a message recorded on cassette tape. Put a stamp on a plain white #10 business envelope (no postage meter), and handwrite the address. Mark the envelope "Personal," and put the cassette tape in it, along with a plain sheet of paper that reads, "Please play this cassette tape in your car on your way home from work." Don't sign it. Your message on the cassette should be something like, "Hi, Mr. Jones. This tape takes only two minutes, and I've got a minute and 57 seconds left. This is Hal Becker from The Becker Group. The last time I spoke to you, you told me that you were interested and that I should get in touch with you, but you have been hard to reach. I want to tell you about the benefits of our program. I'll call you on Friday at 10 a.m. Please drive carefully. Are you wearing your seat belt?"

Common Sense Secret #2. Keep your name alive with "The Rock." You can use mementos to stay in touch with people who have done business with you. Hal suggests that you keep your name in front of them and not out of their thoughts. So what can we do beyond the thank-you note or the call to stay in touch? A company called Successories carries loads of business gifts. Hal chose a rock paperweight with the simple inscription, "Attitude is Everything," which, in his case, is a nice reminder of his sales program.

Common Sense Secret #3. Never give up and always follow through: When you make calls to prospects and clients, you should always follow through until you receive a yes or a no. If they buy from someone else, no problem. But you would like to know why they did not buy from you and if there is a possibility for future business. If there is, mark it down and follow through.

Common Sense Secret #4. Use honesty and the golden rule. You must have integrity and be very easy to deal with. Ask the question, "Would you like to do business with someone like yourself?" Treat other people the way you want to be treated.

With all the basics in hand, common sense, and a good program, you should have no problem being able to line up sales and build a super reputation.

Smart Marketing action plan

1. Make a list of 25 prospects who have shown interest, but with whom you're having trouble getting in touch.

2. Use some of Hal's Common Sense Secrets to get your hard-to-reach prospects' attention.

3. Try to develop some of your own techniques in Hal's creative style.

4. Track the ideas that work best for you.

Chapter 52

Speed up Decision-making

Most problems salespeople face with slow decision-making are self-created, according to David Yoho of Professional Educators, Inc. in Louisville, Kentucky. David feels that we sabotage ourselves when we fail to ask ourselves and our prospects certain questions. If there weren't indecision or procrastination, your services would be purchased from a catalog. Ask yourself two questions to improve your results.

1. Do I control the direction, timing, and conditions of my conversations?

When prospects control the sales conversation, you're unlikely to obtain a meaningful decision. However, controlling the direction, timing, and conditions of conversations doesn't mean controlling, intimidating, or pressuring people. It means asking questions that:

- Define solvable problems.
- Elicit critical facts.
- Create urgency.
- Establish credibility.
- Obtain feelings, opinions, and commitments.

- Determine the content and personalization of your value-added proposal.

2. Do I confuse need and want?

People are more likely to decide quickly when they *need* something. However, people need little more than food, clothing, and shelter. Most everything else is a *want*. It is possible to create urgent wants. Just identify problems and potential solutions that haven't yet occurred to the prospect.

By generating new wants and added value, you can create a unique position for yourself, perhaps as the only acceptable alternative. If you don't create wants and urgency, your prospects will probably decide "not to decide." And the likelihood that prospects will actually retain your services decreases dramatically the longer they procrastinate.

Four key initiatives

Here are four key initiatives that will enable you to speed the decision-making process, boost your closing rate, validate your fee, and reduce your stress level.

1. Know more about your clients than they know about you.

To control the sales conversation, you have to know a lot about your prospect before you propose a course of action. Many of us make the mistake of not having a documented set of questions to ask clients. This is humorous, because we all have questions once we land the assignment.

2. Learn prospects' decision-making criteria.

If you don't know how prospects are going to make a decision, you're less likely to get one. Simply ask, "What criteria are you going to use to make the decision?" or

"What do we have to do to land this assignment?" And always obtain a decision date before sending a proposal.

3. Deliver your recommendations and fees directly to decision-makers.

There are decision-makers and decision-influencers. You need to know who's making and influencing the "if," "when," "who," and "what" decisions.

A good way to ask is, for example, "Barbara, should you decide to retain my services, you and who else will make the final decision?"

4. Ask a sequence of definitive commitment questions that simplify decision-making.

Faster buying decisions are initiated at the moment of first contact. Ask the right questions from the beginning or you're asking for delay. Sometimes, you invest lots of time and money pursuing business when you're out of contention.

Prepare and ask definitive commitment questions after each major point in your proposition. For example, after explaining your methods of investigation and research, ask if your prospect believes that you'll have sufficient information to customize the program.

Smart Marketing action plan

1. Next time you're in a selling situation, determine who is in control.

2. Before a sales call, try to identify the difference between the prospect's *needs* and *wants*.

3. Determine who the real decision-maker is early in the sales call.

4. Determine the process the prospect goes through when making a decision.

Index

Smart Marketing

Other Books and Tapes
by Jeff or Marc Slutsky

Street Fighting: Low Cost Advertising for Your Business
Street Smart Marketing
Street Smart Tele-Selling
How to Get Clients
Street Fighter Marketing
The Toastmaster's Guide to Successful Speaking (coauthored by
    Michael Aun)
Neighborhood Sales Builders (six cassettes and workbook)
Video Series (four VHS videos on marketing and selling)

For availability and fees for speeches and seminars, contact:

Jeff and Marc Slutsky
Street Fighter Marketing, Inc.
467 Waterbury Court
Gahanna, OH 43230
614-337-7474 Fax: 614-337-2233
Web site: www.streetfighter.com
E-mail: streetfitr@aol.com